the power of the gaze

new
literacies

AND DIGITAL EPISTEMOLOGIES

Colin Lankshear, Michele Knobel,
Chris Bigum, and Michael Peters
General Editors

Vol. 20

PETER LANG
New York • Washington, D.C./Baltimore • Bern
Frankfurt am Main • Berlin • Brussels • Vienna • Oxford

Janne Seppänen

the power of the gaze

An Introduction to Visual Literacy

Translated by
Aijaleena Ahonen & Kris Clarke

PETER LANG
New York • Washington, D.C./Baltimore • Bern
Frankfurt am Main • Berlin • Brussels • Vienna • Oxford

Library of Congress Cataloging-in-Publication Data

Seppänen, Janne.
[Katseen voima. English]
The power of the gaze: an introduction to visual literacy / Janne Seppänen.
p. cm. — (New literacies and digital epistemologies; v. 20)
Includes bibliographical references.
1. Visual literacy. I. Title. II. Series.
LB1068.S4613   370.15'23—dc22   2006013154
ISBN 978-0-8204-8139-5
ISSN 1523-9543

Bibliographic information published by **Die Deutsche Bibliothek**.
Die Deutsche Bibliothek lists this publication in the "Deutsche
Nationalbibliografie"; detailed bibliographic data is available
on the Internet at http://dnb.ddb.de/.

The Power of the Gaze was originally published in Finnish by Vastapaino
and The Finnish Youth Research Network
Cover photograph by Risto Vainio

The paper in this book meets the guidelines for permanence and durability
of the Committee on Production Guidelines for Book Longevity
of the Council of Library Resources.

Printed in the United States of America

For SIRI

CONTENTS

ᴈ

ILLUSTRATIONS

ACKNOWLEDGMENTS

MANY OF THE ideas in this book are the result of discussion and collaboration with my colleagues and friends. I am especially indebted to Juha Herkman, Mikko Lehtonen, Olli Löytty, Leena-Maija Rossi, Mika Ripatti, Pertti Vehkalahti, and Esa Väliverronen. They all gave me critical insights and helped to clarify my thinking. My colleagues Risto Kunelius, Mari Maasilta, Ensio Puoskari, and Iiris Ruoho supported me in various ways and willingly lent an ear whenever there was a snag in the editing process.

Pertti Alasuutari, Don Slater, Juha Suoranta, and Frank Webster provided me with good advice and encouraged me to publish my book in English. I am also grateful to Jaana Airaksinen, Mika Elo, Aila Helin, Tommi Hoikkala, Niina Kapanen, Colin Lankshear, Pia Sivenius, Juha Suonpää, and Risto Vainio.

Aijaleena Ahonen and Kris Clarke rendered an incisive and fluent translation, and Pasi Romppanen designed the layout.

FILI (Finnish Literature Information Centre), Finnish Youth Research Network, and the Department of Journalism and Mass Communication at the University of Tampere have generously provided support for the translation of this book.

I would like to thank all those people who have helped me acquire permission to reprint pictures. Every effort has been made to trace the owners of copyrighted material. However, this has been impossible in a few cases. I offer my apologies to any copyright holders whose rights may have been infringed upon unwittingly.

Janne Seppänen

CHAPTER ONE

INTRODUCTION

Wᴴᴇɴ ᴛʜᴇ Sᴏᴠɪᴇᴛ regime collapsed, masses of people charged onto the streets and toppled the statues of Marx, Engels and Lenin from their pedestals. Many were tired of living under the stern look of Lenin, who—from the heights of his plinth and with the helpful assistance of the state police—attempted to make the lives of citizens transparent and controlled. The fall of the statues hardly took anybody by surprise. Any time a regime is overthrown, the visible indicators of power are also shorn off, the images and imageries, the visual orders of power.

Hence, we no longer meet the father figures of revolution in the midst of Eastern European metropolitan centers. Now it is the advertisements of international corporations that address the citizens. They form new visual orders, which perhaps most clearly indicate the direction and depth of the change. People are no longer addressed as socialist fellow citizens or comrades, but as consumers who process their identities through brand name products.

As advertisements took over the townscapes and media publicity of former communist countries, the same imagery became the target of critical consumer movements in traditionally capitalist countries. The movements attempt to undermine the spell of advertising by constructing counter-advertisements (Fig. 1.1). The advertisements of *Nike*, *Coca-Cola* and *Calvin Klein* are interpreted as symbols of global capitalism, consumer hysteria and alienation. The question goes: Has freedom been reduced to simply the liberty to choose one brand from amongst thousands of brands?

Passions indeed surge in the sphere of visual culture. It is not solely a question of just the imagery that directly affects political influence or consuming. Movies, photographs, home videos and computer interfaces contain visual orders that articulate in various ways in people's lives. For example, the characters of advertisements and movies provide identification markers, but people also construct their

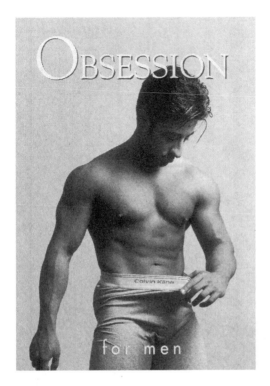

Figure 1.1 *A parody of Calvin Klein's advertisement.*

identities just as much when they pose for a family portrait. All of us process our visibility as well through our outer appearance by the way we dress.

As I sit writing this book, a public debate is raging about the age discrimination—or, perhaps, appearance discrimination is the more correct term—that news anchors and other TV hosts face. Only the young and the attractive seem to qualify for the screen. Sociologist Raija Julkunen (2000) writes in a newspaper article: "The more dynamic and image-sensitive a given industry is, the more difficult it is to connect an aging workforce to it, older women in particular. (...) This era belongs to the young and lean, the signs of success and competence are increasingly written directly on the appearance and body (...) Old people are removed from the public visual world." Julkunen is right on target when she describes one feature connected to visual orders: they draw a line between the visible and the invisible. When certain TV channels want to construct their image, they eliminate aged faces. Hence channels produce a visual order that is based on the visibility of the young and the invisibility of the aged.

Julkunen is not the only one put off by the lopsided public image of women. In the autumn of 2000, Jaana Airaksinen and Niina Kapanen's photographic project *All about My Curves* was completed. The project portrayed quite ordinary and "normal-bodied" women in Polaroid pictures (Fig. 1.2). The photos were put together as an exhibition and a book. The makers of the exhibition described (see Virtanen 2000) how they felt in front of commercial imagery: "When you know what an ideal body looks like, you begin to size up your own body through a very narrow stereotype. After that, you feel inadequate." The idea of the project was to encourage the viewers to accept their own habitus whether or not it fit the ideal measurements.

On the basis of the examples it is possible to form a tentative conception of the notion I pursue through the concept of *visual order*. It refers to *visual reality's regularities and structures, as well as meanings connected to them*. In addition to different pictorial representations, nonverbal communication that takes place by way of the eyes contains visual orders. This includes looks, expressions, appearance and body language. The third area of visual orders is embedded in the physical environment, such as the architectural solutions of buildings and the design of artifacts. All these areas of visual reality contain shared cultural meanings and values which, on their part, enable and, simultaneously, set limits to human activity. For example, people must know how to interpret traffic signs, the facial expressions of their partner in conversation and advertisement pictures in order to be able to live their everyday lives.

The book in your hand provides you with basic tools to understand and analyze different visual orders, regardless of whether they were built on the pictorial

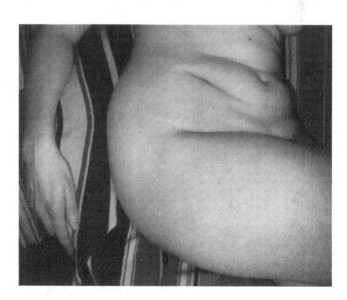

Figure 1.2 *A photograph from the exhibition All About My Curves.* © Copyright Niina Kapanen and Jaana Airaksinen.

representation of media publicity or wordless interaction. Mastery of these tools forms the core of *visual literacy*, which can tentatively be defined as *the skill to understand and critically interpret the function and meanings of different visual representations and orders*. Visual literacy is thus not merely unproblematic learning about visual reality, but also its critical analysis and assessment. It is a different matter to look at, say, an election campaign advertisement when being aware of what means are used in it to address the viewer and how, rather than being blind to them. The understanding of visual orders goes hand in hand with getting a grip on a *look and looking*. Looking is not neutral observation through which the visual stimulants of the surroundings are transmitted to our consciousness. Looking and being the object of a look are in themselves a meaning-mediating social activity which in many ways affects us, or, to put it in the language of research, the construction of our subjectivity.

VISUAL LITERACY AS PART OF LITERACIES

Nowadays, reflections on literacy are often connected to the debate on the information society, which is seen to require new forms of literacies. In 1998, the Finnish Ministry of Education appointed a panel of experts to serve on the Literacy in the Information Society Committee to evaluate the contemporary state and future of literacies. The committee report was submitted in 2000 and outlined several action proposals. The report lists (SOL 2000, 20–21) the following forms of literacy: visual literacy, televisual literacy, computer literacy, intervention literacy, intertextual literacy, technological literacy, multiple literacy, media literacy and internet literacy. The list could be further expanded with much discussed functional, cultural and digital literacies.[1]

The exhaustive list reflects three notions:

First, the concept of literacy is metaphorized to the core. It can, in fact, refer to any skill whatsoever. Computer literacy, for instance, includes technical knowledge of computer hardware and software. The metaphorization of literacy is not a new phenomenon in itself: Sports announcers have throughout time spoken about the skill of reading the game, and it is common to talk about reading a person like an open book. However, along with digital techniques and various new media solutions becoming more common, the use of the concept and meanings of literacy have extensively expanded.

Secondly, the list gives the impression that literacy is means-based, which is to say media-based. Technological literacy requires people to have the skill to understand technical devices well enough to be able to use them in their own everyday lives. Televisual literacy means a good command of the audiovisual language of television. In addition to basic reading skills, the focus of internet literacy is on the use of technology and the skill to navigate the net. Several different literacies are needed in managing a multimedia tool, such as the Internet. The same is valid also for traditional television: one must be able to interpret both the visual images and written or spoken language.

Thirdly, the list reflects a conceptual mess. As it takes on innumerable meanings, the concept of literacy begins to lose its power of distinction. It is well justified to ask what sense it makes to call different practical skills literacies. Why can we not, for instance, simply speak about interpreting of visual images rather than visual literacy?

One reason why I want to hang on to the concept is its clear reference to *learning and studying*—in short, working towards understanding visual reality. Although many visual representations, such as family photos or news pictures, appear to open up to the viewer seemingly naturally, the mechanisms of the formation of their meanings and connections to different visual orders are often hard to see. The skill to detect these meanings, not to mention understanding their function, often demands studies as rigorous as learning to be literate in a foreign language.

In fact, visual literacy became an issue of discussion already in the 1960s. During that time, the International Visual Literacy Association (IVLA), for example, was founded. The IVLA gathered together experts in different fields, such as teachers, photographers, sociologists and psychologists, to discuss the demands that visual culture posed to literacy. The founding of the association was decisively impacted by the breakthrough of television which, it was feared, would undermine children's traditional literacy as a visual medium. The emergence of the problematics of visual literacy was thus connected to the pervasiveness of the new technical invention and the radical cultural change it caused. Similarly, the breakthrough of information technology since the 1990s has raised media fears and, simultaneously, debate on the literacies of the information society.

The necessity of visual literacy has been argued for by the fact that we are living in a "visual era." However, like Mark Poster, a researcher in visual culture, I am not quite certain whether our era is specifically visual, at least in terms of using our sense of sight more than, for example, people who lived in the beginning of the 19th century (see Poster 2002, 62). Certainly they lived in a different visual space than ours and their visual orders were dissimilar, but this does not mean that their reality was in some way less visual than ours. It is very hard to imagine that nonverbal communication would have played a somewhat lesser role in interaction between people then than now. Yet, one thing is clear: the amount of different pictorial representations and media images has indeed explosively increased in the 20th century, and at least people in Western cultures currently live the most pictorial era of their history. In this sense, visual literacy is a quite necessary skill for every person living amidst visual media.

Visual literacy forms a core part of media literacy (on media literacy see Potter 1998), but media form only one area of visual literacy. In this book, I reflect on visual literacy in a larger framework than simply media literacy. Visual literacy therefore also embraces human interaction and nonverbal communication. I also attempt to show that it is essential to understand earlier forms of the pictorial in contemporary digitalized culture. My basic conception is—a little bit paradoxically—conservative and critical: the current digital culture has not necessarily changed those demands that can be set for visual literacy all that much. This is the view that I argue throughout the book with different examples.

It may well be that we are living in an era of social transition, which also sets visual culture into forceful motion. It may also be that the areas of visual culture are changing so rapidly that every attempt to freeze visual culture in the form of a textbook is doomed to fail. I, for one, do not believe this. Continuums are part of history. A functioning analysis of the current state of visual culture, as well as visual literacy itself, demands an understanding of the relationship between cultural change and cultural stability. It is the only way to avoid both the enchantment of digital hype and falling into a rut with outdated ways of seeing.

VISUAL AND VERBAL

The actual task of *The Power of the Gaze* is not to reflect on the relationship between visual orders and verbal *discourses*. However, there is reason to spare a few words on the issue because the concept of visual order is partially derived from theoretical discourse connected to written or spoken language. One aim of my book is to demolish fruitless juxtapositions between the picture and the word, though I am not about to undertake a theoretical or historical analysis of this very intricate question.

A discourse can be defined as a social way of using language which has its own rules and structure both in spoken and written language. An individual grows into language gradually, s/he adopts and savors meanings that language is charged with and learns to use language according to its rules.

In the sphere of social sciences and cultural studies it has become a commonplace to speak about the *linguistic turn*. One sign of this turn is precisely the extraordinary spread of the concept of discourse into different disciplines. The linguistic turn indicates that language has become the most important research target of social sciences and cultural studies during the past couple of decades. Many different theoretical landscapes can be sketched on the background of this linguistic turn, such as Ferdinand de Saussure's structuralist semiotics, Michel Foucault's research and the language philosophies of Peter Winch or Valentin Volosinov.

The aforementioned trends and thinkers share the constructionist notion that language does not merely reflect reality but also constructs it. Language itself becomes a social reality, a meta-individual system which expects every new individual to step inside it. Linguistic reality is by no means random; it has its structures that are connected in many ways to culture, values and attitudes. As s/he learns to speak, a human being steps into the sphere of linguistic system, discourse. This system embraces a number of expressions. However, a person can only express a limited number of states of affairs with them and hence it is said that the boundaries of language are also the boundaries of the world. The current conception of a human being as an actor, a subject, is therefore linguistic or, at the very least, linguistically oriented.

There is no denying that a human being is indeed first and foremost a verbal being. However, a human being is not all about language. The senses of touch, sight, taste and smell transmit our relationship with the outer world. Corporality as a whole plays a significant part in the formation of a person's subjectivity. If a child does not develop a sense of his/her own body, if s/he is never touched, s/he has no better chance to grow into a healthy adult than if s/he was totally isolated from verbal interaction. The focus on language that emerged along with the linguistic turn has thus screened out many other important factors of human life.

The main role of *The Power of the Gaze* is played by a bodily, seeing human being who exists in the sphere of linguistic interaction, but is a sum of much more than that alone. I place an emphasis on the fact that the visual and verbal are not opposites, but they are dimensions of the psyche and culture that are closely interconnected. This can be argued in many ways.

First, in the unconscious layers of the psyche it is almost impossible to separate the verbal and the visual from one another. The 'concepts' that exist in the unconscious are both visual and linguistic figures. Human dreams are manifestations of the unconscious in which the verbal and the pictorial are seamlessly intermingled. The pictorial expressions of dreams can be organized in accordance with the structures of language even if the pictures in themselves are not words. Sigmund Freud indeed used the expression picture writing (*Bilderschrift*) about the contents of a dream.

Secondly, the verbal is also visual on the conscious level of the psyche. Text is read with the eyes, while with words it is possible to build visual spaces and figures.

The famous beginning of Raymond Chandler's *The Big Sleep* (1939) is a forceful example of the construction of visual impressions through the means of text:

> It was about eleven o'clock in the morning, mid-October, with the sun not shining and a look of hard wet rain in the clearness of the foothills. I was wearing my powder-blue suit, with dark shirt, tie and display handkerchief, black brogues, black wool socks with dark blue clocks on them. I was neat, clean, shaved and sober, and I didn't care who knew it. I was everything the well-dressed private detective ought to be. I was calling on four million dollars.[2]

Thirdly, because the verbal is visual, it is logical that the visual is also verbal. Often it is only after I have discussed a movie with someone else that I actually comprehend what I have seen. Hence the use of language makes the experience of pictorial visible; however, much of the experience still remains beyond the reach of language. From this perspective, visual literacy is also the capacity to turn a visual experience into the verbal and communicate it to others.

Sometimes the verbal can be the only way to capture the visual. Jonathan Crary has studied the changes in the ways of observing at the beginning of the 19th century in his much-debated study *Techniques of the Observer* (1990). Crary traced these changes by reflecting on the position of the *camera obscura*, the predecessor of the photographic camera, both as a technical invention and as a metaphor that philosophers used in their texts. The arrangement was elegant. When Crary wanted to find out how the ways of visual perception changed during the course of history, he refrained from studying paintings, drawings or anything at all that was counted in the sphere of the traditionally visual. Instead, he began to trace the formation of the visual in written texts. He asks, for instance, what Goethe's chromatics (*Farbenlehre*) tells about the ways of visual perception of the era. Another researcher on visual culture, Martin Jay works in a very similar way in his massive opus, *Downcast Eyes* (1993), which traces back the meanings of the visual from the thinkers of the Antiquity to the French philosophical discussion at the end of the 20th century.

THE STRUCTURE OF THE BOOK

The aim of this book is not to draw an overview of the development of research on visual culture, which has strongly emerged in the past couple of decades as its own research area. The previously mentioned works of Jay and Crary are central examples of this (see also Walker & Chaplin 1997; Mirzoeff 1999; Sturken & Cartwright 2001; Elkins 2003.) The broad tradition of film and photography research has been nearly totally excised. Art research is not discussed. The bypassing of the important areas of visual culture research certainly does not mean that they would not be necessary in terms of visual literacy. On the contrary, becoming familiar with the different traditions of visual culture research is essential because they provide the means to perceive how visual orders are formed within each pictorial genre, such as the cinema or documentary photograph.

In this book, I begin with concrete everyday situations, visual orders and the problematics of the human being who is both looking and looked at. At times, I use examples from my own life and Nordic culture. These examples have been chosen bearing in mind that they also open up new vistas to a reader unfamiliar with the culture in question. Through the examples I concretize the theoretical discussions connected to visual orders and the look. My point of departure is that the understanding of visual orders and the functioning of the look form the foundation for the development of visual literacy.

The Power of the Gaze proceeds from visual orders to the human being that is looking and the object of looking. Towards the end of the book, I focus my own look on one area of visual literacy, pictorial literacy, and introduce certain semiotic functions that are suitable for the interpretation of the visual. Occasionally, I have whipped up longish endnotes which are not essential to read in order to understand the text proper. They do expand on the definition of some concepts, though, as well as on theoretical discourse connected to them.

In chapter 2, I describe visual orders and construct a theoretical basis for their understanding. Visual orders can be constructed in very personal areas: the object world of the home, family albums or a dress code. They can also be enormously broad, such as French philosopher Jean Baudrillard's vision of simulation, which he understands as a force that controls the visuality of the entire culture. It is impossible to avoid reflections on power in connection with visual orders. I explicate this theme through the famous French theoretician Michel Foucault's ideas. I also go through three stories of the visual representations of culture. I let the voices of classical philosopher Plato and Guy Debord, who developed the theory of the spectacle, as well as the already mentioned Baudrillard, be heard. To comment on these conceptions, I explore certain everyday practices of making pictures, with which people themselves try to have an influence on what kinds of visual orders are produced for the public.

The third chapter focuses on the position of the look and the Gaze in human interaction. To start off the chapter, I clarify certain notions connected to the selectivity of the look. I touch upon the mythology of the eye. I reflect on the look as a social bond between people and as a form of nonverbal communication.

I also attempt to concretize the thoughts about a look, looking and the Gaze of philosopher Jean-Paul Sartre and Jacques Lacan, which are often considered difficult to understand.

In the fourth chapter, I concentrate on the thoughts of Richard Sinatra and Paul Messaris about visual literacy and discuss the relationship between the pictorial (mediated) and immediate (not mediated) perception. I also show how the meanings connected to the traditional camera and photograph also define the image production of the digital era. I reflect on the effects of digitalization on the truth of the photograph, or, to be precise, on how the questions about photographic truth are posed. Finally, I put together a light version of a semiotic tool box in order to analyze pictures.

The Power of the Gaze is written for all readers interested in visual culture and its phenomena. The book is well suited for use as the first textbook on visual culture in universities and teacher training institutions. At times the work may seem a little heavy theoretically, but I do believe that most of the book's thoughts will resonate also for people who have not previously been familiar with the research on visual culture.

CHAPTER TWO

LIVING IN VISUAL ORDERS

I SIT AT MY kitchen table. Across from the table is a cream-colored wall wreathed by a plant left behind by the previous dweller. A low closet door whose upper part curves into a beautiful arch penetrates the wall. Next to the door squats a red easy chair adjoined by a bookcase. The space above the bookcase is dominated by a large, framed photograph by E. A. Bergius: it is Tampere 1954. In the picture I see the house my father once lived in. Occasionally, I slip into the picture and let it take my thoughts back to the past. To the right of the photograph, on the back wall of the kitchen, struts a battery of ugly white kitchen gadgets. I do not exactly want to see them; indeed, to deceive the eye, I have hung a large, black and white poster depicting the rap band Public Enemy on the wall (Fig. 2.1). Saturnine black men glare directly at the camera, the text FEAR OF A BLACK PLANET set in bold letters is positioned on the bottom of the poster. In my current state of mind the poster appears naïve. Why did I buy it in the first place?

The visual countenance of my home is not insignificant. It is part of me; its extension, in fact. My kitchen forms a visual entity which consists of surfaces, doorways, the light that falls from the window, chairs, tables, bookcases and pictures, as well as dozens, if not hundreds, of everyday objects. Most of the time all this is self-evident to me, and actually becomes invisible in its enormous visibility. The old story about hiding an object comes to mind. The first possibility is to dig a deep grave, place the object on the bottom and shovel a solid heap of soil on top of it. If this feels too straightforward, an object can also be hidden amongst others that are exactly the same. It is impossible to find a specific piece of straw from a huge haystack. Movies are abundant with scenes where a wanted person dons a uniform and vanishes into a bevy of other uniforms. The third way of hiding requires the largest amount of skill but is apparently also the most effective. It is possible to place an object in such a visible spot that it transforms into a self-evident part of the visual order of the space and is thus rendered invisible.

Figure 2.1 *The view from the author's kitchen.* Photo by author.

Usually the visual order of my home has to do with the functions of the objects. It is natural that pots and pans are near the faucet and the stove. Yet, how to justify the espresso maker on the windowsill? It has apparently found its place due to its aesthetic nature, not because of its actual function: I do not wish to hide a beautiful artefact from my own gaze or that of my guests. Nowadays I make espresso so seldom that the significance of the pot is perhaps not in its original utility value but as part of the visual countenance of my kitchen. This is not unheard of as people acquire objects for reasons other than their primary function because they are beautiful, extraordinary, or simply look otherwise interesting. In my student days it was quite possible to run across a traffic sign hauled from the street into the bedroom of a friend.

The visual order of my home is awash with meanings, narratives of things and objects which communicate to me, as well as to the occasional visitor, what the person is like who lives here. To some people, their own space is so revealing that the threshold to invite a guest over rises high. Others exhibit their home in earnest, even on the pages of interior design magazines. The apartment of one of my acquaintances is a completeness tuned to perfection; every individual object rests in its designated place, highly polished shoes are arranged in a neat row, the parquet floor lies immaculate in its gloss, carpets, furniture and wall surfaces seamlessly complement each other. The place has been fastidiously constructed piece by piece, sparing not a penny, and indeed it has become a work of art, a manifestation of extraordinary aesthetic taste.

Visual orders can certainly be found elsewhere than between the walls of a home. I live in Tampere, an old Finnish industrial city. Even though the town center continuously metamorphosizes, it forms a relatively settled visual whole. I assume that I have the license to expect that the townscape will not change overnight into something completely different. Tomorrow the most impressive sight on my way to work will be the stadium made of concrete whose towers of light reach up to clouds similar to a gothic church which aspires to spiritual heights. My commute and its visual order create a map in my mind which helps me to plan activities in advance. I can, for instance, ponder what would be the most pleasant route to walk or cycle to work today. Maps depicted in my mind facilitate my movements in the environment.

Visual orders are also the subjects of struggles. For ages a fierce debate has been going on in my hometown about whether a bridge planned to be built in the traditional industrial milieu of the Tammerkoski Rapids would spoil the entire townscape. There are various different sketches and drawings (Fig. 2.2 and 2.3) of the bridge whose qualities are the topic of continuous squabbles.

Figures 2.2–2.3 *The Koskenniska Bridge designed for the Mältinranta area of the Tammerkoski Rapids has raised a great deal of opposition from town dwellers. The bridge has been visually depicted in several different ways. The pair of pictures above is a representation disseminated by the City of Tampere which depicts the 'before and after' stages of the proposed bridge. The pair of pictures below is a representa-*

tion used by the Mältinranta movement, which opposes the construction project, to show the impact that the bridge will have on the townscape. © Copyright pictures above: City of Tampere. © Copyright pictures below: Journalism Research and Development Center, Department of Journalism and Mass Communication, University of Tampere.

Controversies connected to townscapes show how complex the relationship is between visual orders and values, norms and attitudes. Those who admire speed, modernity and metropolises see no problem in building high rises in the city center. Those who take a stand for low rise cityscapes see the same buildings as a rape of tradition, and thus, of history itself.

The eye also accommodates itself to visual orders. Over twenty years ago a shopping center and a tall hotel were built to replace the old industrial milieu that formerly dominated that particular part of town. Even with the best of intentions one can not claim that the constructions please the eye—to use a worn expression. I clearly remember the upset when the revelation hit me: this is what the city center will look like from now on at this particular spot. Nowadays I hardly pay attention to the fact. The buildings have become a self-evident part of the city's visual order, regardless of the dispute surrounding them during the time of their creation. I might be upset again if one morning they disappeared.

A visual order can refer to the object world of our living environment, its established features and their meanings, as was the case in the examples above. Similarly, a visual order can incorporated in a pictorial representation. Photographs, movies, advertisements, drawings and television programs all contain more or less established means of visual representation—in two interlocking ways, in fact. First, the medium itself contains visual orders. For instance, there are plenty of cultural meanings attached to a photograph through which we interpret its messages. A photograph is considered more truthful than, for example, a drawing in pencil; or at least we evaluate photographs more easily from the viewpoint of truthfulness. The meanings of a visual representation connected to its genre and medium are therefore intertwined as part of its visual order. Secondly, orders can be linked with the represented subjects and the ways they are represented. Very important visual orders are connected, for instance, with the ways that gender, ethnic minorities or even foreign countries are represented. Are the realities of the countries of the African continent reduced to negative images of famine, wars and AIDS victims?

- The visual is thus not merely an arbitrary flow of visual sensations. Structures and orders are formed in it. These visual orders can be found both in the physical environment, the object world, and in the forms and contents of representations.[1]

All of these orders are always a consequence of human activity. First of all, people produce them by creating new visual objects—pictures and other artefacts. Secondly, people interpret these objects more or less consciously and link them as part of their own activities and familiar meanings. Interpreting visual objects also means creating them. The order in an intact natural landscape is not created before a human being interprets nature. Of course it can be claimed that the physical and biological cycles of nature have existed long before human beings, and that they are very orderly and also visible at least for certain animal species. True enough, but they enter the realm of visual orders only when the rhythms of nature are interwoven as part of activity that includes human meanings; namely, culture.

Visual orders can also be found in established ways of looking, that is, the physiology of seeing and cultural norms. We reach the physical barriers of seeing fairly quickly: the eye is confined to perceiving only a relatively narrow slice of the wavelengths of electro-magnetic radiation and the field of vision as well as its capacity to discern objects from one another is limited. In regard to visual orders, however, the norms that shape gaze and looking are more essential. In Western culture it is polite to look straight into the eyes of the partner in conversation, but a lingering look quickly becomes staring. In certain cultures it is inappropriate to look into the eyes of one's senior. Voyeurism is usually socially reprehensible, though the peephole and surveillance camera tend to be exceptions.

- Interaction that relies on gaze contains visual orders. Looking is a normative activity that communicates meanings.

Visual order is always an outcome of human activity: a human being molds and constructs one's visual surroundings and makes visual representations in different social practices. For instance, taking news photographs is called journalism and is usually handled by photographers following their own professional practices. Before finding its place on the page of a newspaper, a photograph has potentially visited the user interface of a photo editor or a reporter. They may have manipulated the photo in various ways. The person responsible for the layout, often a professional graphic designer, decides where the photo is placed on the page of the paper. All of these people are bound by publicly expressed or unspoken agreements that are more or less connected to journalistic practice. These agreements have an impact on what the visual order is like on the pages of the paper; what is shown and what is omitted.

- Visual orders are functional and material orders which are articulated into the activities of different institutions.

All said above can be condensed into perhaps the most important feature of visual orders:

- Visual orders contain established and shared cultural meanings.

PICTURES ARE PART OF THE VISUAL

All reality that is accessible with sight is visual. Hence *visible* can be considered a parallel term. A little more flexible definition allows dreams, fantasies in the waking state and delusions to be included in the sphere of visual; as well as many linguistic expressions that may be very visual indeed. Thus, the visual has metamorphosed as part of language; it is an intrinsic part of language. In English—and in Finnish—we commonly use, for instance, the following expressions: to see through someone else's eyes, to focus on the essential, your eyes are bigger than your stomach, to have a point of view, or to place oneself above others. Any language has heaps of such expressions; the English *to see* being perhaps the best known for its double meaning of both *to behold* and *to comprehend.*

Even though the visual and the linguistic overlap in many ways, a human being can have visual experiences that cannot be analyzed through a linguistic system. We can perceive and recognize a remarkably larger number of colors than we can name. A certain painting can provoke emotional states in us of which only a small part can be translated into linguistic expression. The outward appearance of another person can stir the desire to meet him or her, or an antipathy that is just as strong. Language reaches, if and when it does, only a small part of these kinds of meanings.

Words stream out of the mouth, but they can also spring from the hands; as writing or sign language. People hear speech with their ears, but they can also read words with their eyes or skin. Speech has rhythm, and sometimes words can conspire with music and seduce the whole body into motion. Words can also be written in handwriting that attunes the eye to beauty or graphological interpretation. Language indeed is absorbed into a human being and radiates from a human being through the entire spectrum of sensuality. We can touch, hear, taste, and see words. From the sensory perspective, language reaches far beyond mere eyesight. A visual sensation, though, can also be created by stimulating the optic nerve or the sight centre in the brain: a blow on a head can make one 'see stars'. Moreover, an image drawn on the skin with a finger can be sensed as a picture.

The meanings of the visual and pictorial oscillate near one another, but their relationship is asymmetrical. All pictorial is visual, but not all visual is pictorial. However, the line between them is blurred for two reasons. First of all, insofar as a visual sensation is linked to the eye it is always based on a picture because what is depicted on the retina is a picture. Secondly, objects, which we are not used to being regarded as pictures, are always pictorial. They are three-dimensional representations in themselves. However, I constrain the pictorial to mean only pictorial representations; in other words, photographs, drawings, computerized images, paintings (figurative and non-figurative), cartoons and so forth. When I talk about the pictorial I mean the two-dimensionally visual.

Visual orders are therefore meaningful orders. They include expectations, norms, emotions, and are an essential part of human interaction. I cannot appear at a funeral clad in a t-shirt. I do not have the absolute power to decide what color I paint my house because the building authorities have a legal right to have their say. Moreover, an individual, such as a business executive, Somali or a homosexual, is categorized on the basis of his or her outward appearance.

Visual orders have always existed. For people who lived in hunter and gatherer societies the predictability of the visual environment was a significant matter: plants and animals hardly change their appearance, at least not during the lifetime of one generation. Their recognition required visual literacy. One had to be able to discern edible species from toxic ones—this is still a precondition for safety when we gather mushrooms in the forest. We must know what a poisonous mushroom looks like.

During the past hundred years Western visual orders have been shaken up in a way that could be characterized as *the breakthrough of the pictorial.* Pictures have been important for people ever since prehistoric cave paintings, but only during the 20ᵗʰ century did the production of pictorial expand by remarkable dimensions. Certain inventions, such as photography, the halftone process and printing techniques, movies, television, and lastly the user interface of the computer have had a decisive impact on this. But first and foremost it was the development of mass production, consumerism and modern publicity that caused the expansion of the pictorial. Marketing goods through images has produced a massive domain of the pictorial that is largely focused on pictorial advertising, the packaging of the goods and the aesthetic honing of the goods themselves. Publicity, in its turn, has been filled to the brim with consumer advertisements. Meanwhile newspapers, magazines and journals, different pictorial works of art, photographs, movies and many other media that contain pictorial elements have been molded into marketable goods and entertainment. We can also include in the domain of the pictorial all of the innumerable surveillance and control applications, such as cameras targeted at citizens in shops, public offices and streets that enhance people's overall visibility.

The pictorial has without doubt developed into the dominating field of the visual in which many kinds of visual orders are constructed. It may well be that the pictorial has started to live its own life as a spectacle. It has grown into a kind of a reality in itself, and is finally straining against its own limited scope. The merely pictorial is no longer satisfactory, but a more comprehensive sensory experience is demanded: virtual reality. A three-dimensional and interactive visual space is created and its resemblance to reality is augmented by adding audio landscape or, possibly, by manipulating the sense of touch. For now the creation of virtual realities is only in its initial phase and actual functioning applications are still embryonic.

THE VISUAL IS MULTIMODAL

The contemporary visual is seldom purely pictorial. Movies are not only watched, they are also listened to and read. The traditional film creates its world through both the auditory and visual means. Meanings in a film are thus communicated through several different meaning-giving systems, or to put it semiotically, through *codes*. They are multimodal means of expression.[2]

Photographs are also often accompanied by text. Newspapers hardly ever publish photographs without captions. For instance, Ronald Barthes (1915–1980) thought that the caption anchors the meanings of a photograph in their place. However, we can just as well think that it is actually the photograph that anchors the meaning of the caption. It is not very hard at all to construct situations where the same caption illustrated with a different picture takes on quite opposite meanings. Let's imagine Politician N.N. speaking to an audience: Caption: 'N.N.'s speech was enthusiastically received.' The first photo is taken from amongst the audience. It depicts N.N. promoting his message. The other photo is taken diagonally from behind. N.N.'s side profile is in the photograph, but the largest part of the picture surface is dominated by a view to a vast conference hall where a half-dozen blasé listeners slouch in their chairs. In the latter case the photo directs the caption towards irony of which there is not even an inkling in the first case.

The pictorial is interwoven with other senses and code systems, as well as the experience we receive through them of the world, the individual body, psychological states, images and emotions. It is hard to estimate how large will be the impact of the new user interfaces on the increase of multimodality. Perhaps different representations have always been multimodal, but only now have we started to pay more attention to their multimodality. My own 'multimodal' experience from the end of the 1960s comes to mind.

I was incredibly excited about the Finnish writer Väinö Linna's wartime epic *The Unknown Soldier* and read the novel again and again. For a boy verging on puberty *The Unknown* was a superb tale of male bonding and the sharing of a common experience. It provided a vast emotional scale of joy, fear, sorrow, human folly and strength without neglecting the thin but significant line that exists between the worlds of the adult male characters of the book and the young boy reading it. *The Unknown* that we had in the house was the so-called folk edition which was illustrated with still pictures from the movie version of the novel directed by Edvin Laine. I had not yet seen the film, but in my mind those images were so tightly glued to the narrative of the novel that they began to live along with the novel as visual characters. I constructed my own movie of them, and ever since the characters of Rokka, Hietanen and Lehto have refused to be separated from these visual forms of themselves. For the majority of Finns, *The Unknown* is expressly a visual-literal experience in which Laine's movie and Linna's novel are irrevocably intermingled. They are furthermore bound together with the historical situation: post-war Finland of the 1950s and the task that fell on both of these works of art to re-narrate the experiences of war in the minds of the generation that was there and lived through it.

Later in life I discussed both the novel and the film of *The Unknown* with a war veteran. He remarked that "that is exactly how it was there." I did not believe him, and only later did I understand in which sense the remark was more than true. *The Unknown* had become a story that made the senseless comprehensible. *The Unknown* is a good example of how fantasy, reality, pictures, texts and images articulate and construct a socially and nationally significant history.

In this sense multimodality is not a matter connected only to digital culture, even though the user interface of a computer has become its metaphor, and never before in conjunction with the development of the information society has the entire phenomenon become a subject of thorough study. The images in cartoons, books and films interweave. Pictorial and textual solutions in advertisements, even listening to the radio and reading a paper at the same time, are multimodal ways of experiencing. Multimodality is an essential feature of popular culture and, at the same time, human experience.

POWER—THAT FORCE OF ALL TRADES

Where there is social order there is also power, and because visual orders are social orders, power is an inseparable part of their activity. The authorities have actual power to influence what the visual space and countenance of a city become like. Cities have architects who give official statements about whether a planned building suits the townscape or not. In the city center as well as in areas categorized as having historical value the visual countenance of a building is scrutinized particularly closely. Indeed it is prevailing practice that the applicant for a building license negotiates with the authorities in these kinds of cases already before submitting the license application. Various things are assessed: construction masses, frontage treatment, materials, colors, the positioning of possible ads, hoardings and signs. Power is present in many ways also in zoning, town planning, the planning of parks and streetside greenery. An appropriate committee makes the final judgments that have an impact on the visual order.

The visual orders of cities are indeed highly regulated. It is a different matter altogether what kinds of visual solutions are seen to be worthy of promotion, which are rejected, and on what grounds. And how are the needs and expectations of the inhabitants realized when decisions are made about changing the townscape? If the aim is to minimize building costs and maximize financial profit, there is no reason to invest many intellectual and financial resources in the visual appearance. The visual order of a town, the financial variables of construction, the general principles of business operations, town planning policies and value judgments of different tastes in concern of the townscape form a complex network of power relationships. Each and every resident of the town can evaluate the end result of its activity afterwards as they glance around their environment.

The police are wardens not only of public order, but also visual orders. It is not uncommon that before state visits the target places are purged of elements that offend the eyes of the guests and are a source of shame for the hosts, such as winos and the homeless. For the same reason roads can be newly paved, parks replanted and buildings given a makeover. At times authorities think that also the ordinary people should be protected from harmful imagery, as happened in Jyväskylä, Finland, in Easter of 2000. The police banned the showing of all movies rated 16 on Maundy Thursday through the following Saturday. The ban applied to *Scream 3*, *Sleepy Hollow* and the Finnish film *The Restless*. In Finland's largest daily newspaper, *Helsingin Sanomat*, the police justified their activity by stating that the movies concerned were not fit for 'families' to watch at Easter time due to 'their violent and indecent content'.[3] The authorities also often face the tedious waste of their time on those who choose to challenge the prevalent visual order and spray paint an artful graffiti on a grey slab of concrete or taint a newly-painted Jugendstil house with an indecipherable mess.

The visual order of a town is hence intimately linked official and unofficial regulations, customs and norms where power concentrates and defines the borders between the permissible and the prohibited, the possible and the impossible.

The power connected to visual orders is not only restrictive, even though the police can indeed clean up the townscape or city block, and even the screening of films. French historian and philosopher Michel Foucault (1926–1984) emphasizes the productivity of power. He (1986, 156) states:

It's a machine in which everyone is caught, those who exercise power just as much as those over which it is exercised (…) Power is no longer substantially identified with an individual who possesses or exercises it by right of birth; it becomes a machinery that no one owns. Certainly everyone doesn't occupy the same position; certain positions preponderate and permit an effect of supremacy to be produced.

Power works when people adapt themselves to visual orders, interpret them in certain ways and begin to see them as self-evident and unquestionable.

For Foucault, one essential dimension of power is visibility: an individual is easily controlled if his or her visibility can be guaranteed. "Visibility is a trap", he (Foucault 1977, 200) notes. People's visibility can be enhanced through architectural solutions, camera applications, the seating order in a classroom and so forth. However, the demand for visibility can be extended far deeper than that. In security checks at airports luggage is transilluminated; in other words, advanced camera technology is used *to see* what the given passenger intends to send off into the cargo hold. This kind of exercise of power, which is based on visibility and a gaze that penetrates deep, is essentially accepted by both the controller and the controlled because it takes place in the name of public safety. Perhaps the productivity of power becomes even more apparent in the ordinary line to the cashier at a supermarket. A kind note is attached to many cash registers: "Please open your bag for the sake of mutual trust". The request is obviously contradictory because it proves in itself that there is no trust. Each and every customer is a potential thief. I have sometimes observed how many are the people who actually comply and open their bags to be checked by the cashier. It even appears that quite a number of people have the need to prove that they belong to the troops of the honest. People are *voluntarily* willing to open a bit of their private lives to be scanned by a controlling gaze. It is precisely this willingness that must possess something essential in regard to visibility and Foucauldian power. The more willing individuals are to expose themselves to the controlling gaze, to make themselves transparent, the easier it is to control them. Maybe the most enthused bag-openers have internalized the controlling gaze so completely that they themselves have grown a tiny surveillance camera in some nook of their minds. This theme of the relationship between gaze, power and human activity is intriguing, and I return to it, as well as to Foucault, in the next chapter.

Even though visibility is essential in terms of the operation of power, invisibility is just as important. Just as in linguistic interaction where it is important what is said and what not, in visual interaction and representations it is important what is not seen. Invisibility is exclusion from the visual order. Newspapers relatively seldom publicize pictures of members of the social margins—such as disabled people or sexual and ethnic minorities. One means of marginalizing these people is precisely to make them invisible one way or another. Hence, through exclusion, imagery constructs the norm of normal and desired humanity and the visual order that maintains it.

An essential matter regarding power is also what kind of imagery people feel the desire to identify themselves with. There has been much public discourse about whether the emaciated female images of advertising have an impact on the increase in eating disorders among women and young girls. The question encompasses the notion that girls identify themselves with the visual order of the female body that advertising reinforces. It is unclear what the exact connection is between this kind of identification and eating disorders, but it is certain that advertising provides both genders identification markers connected to physical appearance. Here, power functions as the aspect of which kinds of bodily representations are preferred and desirable, and which are rejected. In this respect the imagery of advertising upholds general visual orders connected to appearance. In these orders, people are graded into categories such as fat, thin and normal.

SEEING HAS CULTURAL PRECONDITIONS

The concept of visual order used in this book draws partly from the research that has developed since the 1970s which analyses the cultural preconditions of looking and seeing. These studies have often been inspired by the notion that during different eras of history, certain kinds of different grand visual orders (ways of perceiving the visible) have prevailed. The problematic of the linear perspective of the Renaissance and the relationship of the perceiving subject and the perceived object connected to it is often found at the core of the research. One of the most influential works in the field is *Ways of Seeing* (1972) by British author and researcher on visual culture John Berger. Significant texts that explore ways of seeing include studies on visual culture by Martin Jay (1988; 1993) and Jonathan Crary (1988; 1990). The objective of this book is not to focus on the history of ways of seeing, however there is reason to take a brief look at the problematics of the linear or the Cartesian perspective.

As can be deduced from the expression itself, the Cartesian perspective is connected to both the philosophy of René Descartes (1596–1650) and the linear perspective familiar from the art of painting. The linear perspective is a way of representation which developed within the visual art of the Renaissance. It is a visual order used to create an effect of depth and space in paintings. In a painting where the linear perspective is applied, parallel lines meet in the horizon—in the vanishing point—and objects that are closer are depicted larger than those further away. Filippo Brunelleschi (1377–1446) most often gets the credit for discovering the mathematical laws of the linear perspective. Among the first publications that discussed the linear perspective were Leon Battista Alberti's (1404–1472) *Della pittura* (1436), Piero della Francesca's (1420–1492) *De prospectiva pingendi* (1480) and Albrecht Dürer's (1471–1528) *Underweysung der Messung*. Dürer also invented the famous grid (Fig. 2.4), through which a painter could draw an accurate figure of his object in terms of perspective.

Figure 2.4 *Albrecht Dürer's drawing circa 1525.*

The linear perspective is said to have made it possible for the art of painting to be realistic. However, as Mikko Lehtonen (1994, 120) remarks, what was overlooked in the underlying assumptions of the linear perspective "to represent the world as it is" is that the linear perspective itself is only one possible way of perceiving reality. As a matter of fact, the linear perspective corresponds only partially to the natural way of seeing. A human being sees everything through two eyes, but the linear perspective has only one point of vision. The field of vision is not consistent in the same way as the rules of the linear perspective which continue into the horizon with mathematical exactness. Moreover, perspective ties the viewer of a painting to a stationary point, indeed precisely to the very point from which the painter perceives the picture. This does not correspond to a normal situation where the viewer can move about. Already on these grounds the realistic quality of the linear perspective is questionable. The linear perspective produced—and continues to produce—a motionless and disembodied visual angle on its object. It is as if the painter's gaze captures the flux of phenomena and perceives the visual field from a privileged point of view outside any motion taking place in it. In short, it is as if the viewer were not there at all. This point of view overlooked the fact that the viewer is always positioned somewhere and that the human visual angle is always limited. (*Ibid.*, 212)

But how does this connect with the philosophy of Descartes?

According to Descartes, the senses and the body cannot be sources of reliable knowledge. It is possible to achieve genuine knowledge only through separation from the bodily and solely focus on the power of the enlightened mind, disconnected from debris of the sensory. Even though the linear perspective is connected to sensory experience—namely, sight—it is nevertheless a mathematically precise relationship with the world; calculated by the mind. Thanks to this, it actually controls sensory experience; and even reaches beyond it. It disciplines sight and forges it to fit the framework of reason. Moreover, as perspective distinguishes the perceiving subject from the perceived object, it corresponds with the preconditions of the formation of Cartesian knowledge even in a broader sense. Lehtonen (*ibid.*, 127) compresses the notion:

> Cartesian perspectivism is characterized by its lonely eye, like the eye of a Cyclops, which perceives reality outside itself; something in which it is not included. Similarly, the eye itself is conceived to be static, attached to something, anything but dynamic. In the Cartesian perspective, seeing—seeing by a Cyclops bound to one place—is not mobile seeing but arrested gaze. It is immortalized, idealized, detached from the body, coldly abstract, a non-participatory gaze. Moreover, it is gaze that does not see itself. Being positioned outside the field of vision inhibits the seer from seeing him or herself as the producer of the scene.

Cartesian perspectivism has also been part of modern science, or rather, part of the ideology of science. According to it, the researcher is always an observer separated from his object who himself has no influence over the studied topic. The researcher has become an observer of the world instead of being a participant in it. We can safely note that we run into Cartesian perspectivism always when the one-way, observing relationship of a researcher or perceiver to the observed object is underlined.

What was said above may give the reader the impression that Cartesian perspectivism has been the prevailing way of seeing. However, it is very difficult to say how strong the position of the linear perspective or Cartesian perspectivism has been in the history of Western civilization. Research on the topic largely relies on the traditions of the art of painting and philosophy. This raises many questions. How was the world perceived outside these cultural domains? What ways of seeing prevailed amongst the quite common, illiterate hoi polloi who never saw a painting—with the exception, perhaps, of religious images?

In any case, there was clearly an understanding about the conventional quality of the linear perspective already at the same time that people began to master its usage. The interest in so-called anamorphoses, which were enthusiastically studied in the 16th and 17th centuries, may illuminate the notion (Sivenius 1997). An anamorphosis (Fig. 2.5) is an optical toy of sorts which at first sight looks like a mishmash of lines and forms, but when looked at from a certain angle, its illegible chaos unfolds into a clear image. An anamorphosis poses a challenge to the viewer, because he has to discover the correct angle of viewing through trial and error. An anamorphosis thus emphasizes the mobility of the viewer which does not correspond with the idea of the linear perspective.

The anamorphosis also found its way into the painting *The Ambassadors* (1533) by Hans Holbein (1497–1543). (Fig. 2.6) When the painting is examined straight from the front, the geometrical point, everything seems clear. The painting portrays two men leaning on a tall table on which lies a collection of artefacts. The history of the painting reveals that it represents two potentates of the time, Jean de Dinteville and Georges de Selve. The objects on the table, such as the globe and lute, symbolize science and the arts. However, the mind of the viewer becomes occupied with an oval-shaped patch on the bottom of the painting which does

Figure 2.5 *An anamorphic picture and cylinder.* Photograph © Copyright Mika Elo.

not seem to make much sense. Indeed, when viewed from the geometrical point the figure is impossible to recognize. The patch is an anamorphosis and the viewer must move away from the geometrical point to realize that it is actually a skull. It is quite clear when standing in front of this kind of painting that the notion of the scene controlled by the viewer is nothing if not questionable. Through its own pictorial quality, the painting shows how artificial the position of the viewer actually is. The viewer must step away to the side the painting to be able to discern the skull. Holbein was certainly aware of this as he was working on the portrait. The extraordinary painting has generated a great deal of discussion.

Martin Jay (1988) calls the Cartesian perspective a *scopic regime*, a concept originally introduced by film theorist Christian Metz. According to Jay, there is no single scopic area that totally determines the visual, and in characterizing the multiplicity of the ways of seeing he uses the expression *polyscopic*. Translated into the language of this book, we can say that there are several different and possibly rivaling visual orders. Towards the end of this chapter I introduce a few examples.

To summarize what was said above, we can conclude that the essential domains in terms of visual orders are:

Figure 2.6
Hans Holbein's 1533 painting The Ambassadors. *At the forefront of the picture is an anamorphic picture of a skull that becomes recognizable to the eye only when the spectator moves to the side of the painting to look at it.*

- forms and contents of visual representations.
- forms and contents of non-verbal interaction built on the gaze.
- visual structures of the object world.
- cultural norms and ways of seeing that determine the gaze and looking.

All these spheres of visual orders are—to repeat the essential—saturated with meanings. The physical and pictorial elements of the environment form visual orders only on the condition that they contain crystallizations of cultural meanings that are part and parcel of all human activity.

Regardless of the multiplicity of visual reality, many thinkers tend to see totally dominating, even demonic orders. Can it be anything other than historical irony that many totalizing concepts have arisen simultaneously with the expansion and mushrooming of pictorial culture? Good examples are Guy Debord's notion of a *society of spectacle* and Jean Baudrillard's even wilder ideas of *simulation* and the *hyperreal*. However, the conceptions of the pictorial born already in the philosophy of antiquity are an important part of the background of these French simulators. Before dealing with the notions of Debord and Baudrillard, we'll stay a moment in the company of the ancient Greek philosopher Plato (427–347).

THREE TALES OF THE VISUAL

Plato's Wavering Shadows

In Greek Antiquity, sight was considered to be the most important sense. Many of the central myths of Antiquity are drawn from sensations of seeing. One of the best known is the myth of Narcissus, the son of nymph Leiriope and the River-god Cephisus.

Most young boys and maidens became enamored with Narcissus because of his extraordinary beauty, but their love of the self-absorbed youngster remained unconsummated. Particularly persistent in her infatuation was the nymph Echo, who—due to the punishment meted out by the Gods—was not able to speak but could only repeat the last words of the people she heard talk. Hence, she was incapable of expressing her feelings and withered away in her unrequited love until only her voice remained. A young boy who had closely observed Narcissus' behavior, and was angered by it, called on the Gods for vengeance on the arrogant youth. One day after a stroll in the woods Narcissus bent over a spring to quench his thirst. When he saw his reflection on the shimmering water, he became so enraptured by the sight that he could not force himself to leave and starved to death. Narcissus became a prisoner of his own image. Narcissus has lived on through our times in the concept of narcissism and even mundane speculations on human identity, in which the role of other people—mirrors, in a sense—is central. But the myth is also a manifestation of the power of an image, its awesome capacity to stare back at the viewer and capture him in its grip.

In addition to mythology, the regard that the Ancient Greeks had for sight is apparent in philosophy (Jay 1993, 24). Plato discussed the meaning of seeing in many of his dialogues. *Timaeus* examines the order of being. Here Plato develops his cosmological ideas through the dialogue. As the dialogue proceeds, it also runs into the question of the meaning of sight, which indeed becomes the most important human sense because sight makes it possible to understand the universe itself. "But now the sight of day and night, and the months and the revolutions of the years, have created number, and have given us a conception of time, and the power of enquiring about the nature of the universe; and from this source we have derived philosophy, than which no greater good ever was or will be given by the gods to mortal man."[4]

Through sight, it is possible to examine "the courses of intelligence in the heaven" and apply what we see to the movements of our own reason, which are related to the movements on the sky even if less complete. Through the eyes, a human being can thus sense the harmony of the entire universe.

However, the best known of Plato's elaborations of seeing can be found in the den metaphor in the seventh book of *The Republic*. Socrates describes the den in the following way:

> And now, I said, let me show in a figure how far our nature is enlightened or unenlightened: Behold! Human beings living in an underground den, which has a mouth open towards the light and reaching all along the den; here they have been from their childhood, and have their legs and necks chained so that they cannot move, and can only see before them, being prevented by the chains from turning round their heads. Above and behind them a fire is blazing at a distance, and between the fire and the prisoners there is a raised way; and you will see, if you look, a low wall built along the way, like the screen which marionette players have in front of them, over which they show the puppets.

The viewers are only able to see the shadow silhouettes of the performers on the "screen" that the back wall of the den provides. Because the viewers have never seen anything but those obscure images, they have begun to think of them as the only reality. When the prisoners of the den discuss the shadows, they perceive that they are discussing real objects. Socrates continues his metaphor and asks his listeners to imagine what would happen if a captive of the den was suddenly released from his shackles, turned his head and possibly walked out of his prison.

> And now look again, and see what will naturally follow if the prisoners are released and disabused of their terror. At first, when any of them is liberated and compelled suddenly to stand up and turn his neck round and walk and look towards the light, he will suffer sharp pains; the glare will distress him, and he will be unable to see the realities of which in his former state he had seen the shadows; and then conceive someone saying to him, that what he saw before was an illusion, but that now, when he is approaching nearer to being and his eyes turned towards more real existence, he has a clearer vision, what will be his reply?

Socrates answers his own question by guessing that "will he not be perplexed? Will he not fancy that the shadows which he formerly saw are truer than the objects which are now shown to him?"

Socrates considers the temporary blindness caused by the light of the truth a small price for a human being to be liberated from ignorance and the delusionary consciousness shadow images can offer. He believes that through education it is possible for people to turn to the light.

In order to fully understand Plato's metaphor, it must be examined in the context of the central theme of the whole *Republic* dialogue; namely, the question of justice. In what way should the republic be organized so that it could guarantee the greatest possible fairness and justice to its citizens, and through that, happiness? Plato was of the opinion that this kind of ideal republic should be led by philosophers dedicated to the search for truth and good. It would be their task to pilot the state and its citizens towards justice, truth and the good.

But what is the "good"?

Towards the end of the sixth book of the *Republic*, Socrates, accompanied by his mate in conversation, Glaukon, deliberates seeing, light and knowledge. The philosopher asks what more does seeing need than the eye and the objects, and replies: light, that is, the sun. In a certain sense it can be understood that the ability to see flows from the sun into the eye:"Then the sun is not sight, but the author of sight who is recognised by sight." "And this is he whom I call the child of the good, whom the good begat in his own likeness, to be in the visible world, in relation to sight and the things of sight, what the good is in the intellectual world in relation to mind and the things of mind."

When a human being looks at objects on which light no longer flows, he becomes blind, but when light returns and re-illuminates the objects, they are again clearly shown. The good relates to knowledge in a similar fashion. Socrates concludes:

> Now, that which imparts truth to the known and the power of knowing to the knower is
> what I would have you term the idea of good, and this you will deem to be the cause of
> science, and of truth in so far as the latter becomes the subject of knowledge; beautiful too,
> as are both truth and knowledge, you will be right in esteeming this other nature as more
> beautiful that either; and, as in the previous instance, light and sight may be truly said to
> be like the sun, and yet not to be the sun, so in this other sphere, science and truth may be
> deemed to be like the good, but not the good; the good has a place of honor yet higher.

The good is part of knowledge and truth, but it is also much more: the very origin
of knowledge and truth. Hence, the leaders of ideal states, philosophers, must seek
to reach the good because it enables the search for knowledge and truth. On the
other hand, through seeking the truth it is possible to approach the good.

When reading Plato's metaphor it is important to keep in mind his doctrine
of ideas, according to which the visible world is merely an imperfect reflection of
the world of ideas. Though Plato uses seeing as a metaphor for the search of real
truth, he did not trust mere eyesight. Plato's reality divided into two parts, the
visible and that which could only be achieved via thought. The visible consisted
of objects and their images; the part reached through embraced mathematical
truths and the world of ideas. Knowledge concerning the visible was not de facto
knowledge, but closer to beliefs. It was only possible to reach out to the real
light of knowledge through thought, by turning away from the visible and il-
lusionary world of objects and their images. Thus, the den metaphor must not
be understood in such a way that by turning his head towards material objects
in place of their shadow silhouettes a human being would reach the threshold of
real knowledge. The analogy is only superficially about objects and their images;
the relationship between the perceiver and the perceived. The capacity of thought
to go beyond and above the visible world is much more essential. Even though
seeing is metaphorically significant to Plato, he does not rate concrete seeing very
highly as a means to real knowledge. In this sense copies are the most mendacious
representations of all. "Would you not admit that both the sections of this division
have different degrees of truth, and that the copy is to the original as the sphere of
opinion is to the sphere of knowledge?", Socrates demands from his conversation
mate. By "the original of the copy" Socrates does not refer to the world of ideas
but to common material objects, which—similar to pictures—also belong to the
visible world and are only a trifle more real than their images.

Thus, Plato's relationship with sight and the domain of the visible is ambiguous. On the one hand, seeing for him means quite concrete seeing with eyes,
such as perceiving the movements of the heavenly bodies. As such, seeing may
open a splendid path to philosophical truths as well as a fallacy that mocks real

knowledge. In addition to this concrete perceiving, seeing is also metaphorical seeing that could be crystallized in the expression *to see with thought*. According to Martin Jay (1993), this split into two seeings is one central feature connected to the modern and its eye-centeredness. As a matter of fact, the split is apparent even in quite everyday thinking: the expression "I see with the eyes of my soul" expressly points out how a human being can actually see things even with eyes closed, or assisted with the capacity to imagine. When someone sees into the future, he constructs images of possible states of the future with the means of his capacity of thought.

Even if one does not accept Plato's doctrine of ideas, it is possible to discover valuable elements in regard to visual literacy in his critique of the visual and doubts about the knowledge provided by eyesight. Questioning the pictorial and even the meanings of the everyday object world is also an essential dimension of visual literacy. Hence—paradoxically—closing the eyes and using the capacity of thought has become a central part of visual literacy. Plato's den can also be understood as an allegory about being seized up in conventional visual orders. Turning one's head, stepping out of the den and being blinded all refer to the sensation people experience when they begin to approach, if not truth itself, at least ways to understand better what they see.

Debord's Evil Spectacle

Many cultural critics have followed in Plato's footsteps. They have thought that the pictorial and particularly images of advertising alienate people from real life. In the famously critical 1960s people began to talk about *the society of spectacle*. The concept was introduced by French philosopher Guy Debord, who attempted to piece together a kind of grand story of the visual; the prevailing function of visual orders. In 1967, Debord published *La Société du spectacle*, in which he presented his central and often bewilderingly complex theses. In addition to Raoul Vaneigem's texts, Debord's tome became the central theoretical writing of the so-called situationistic movement.

The Situationist International (*L'Internationale Situationniste*) was founded in France ten years before the publication of Debord's book. The group published twelve issues of the magazine *Internationale Situationniste* where Debord was the editor-in-chief. The situationists were largely Marxists who passionately discussed and wrote about Hegel, Marx, and Lukács. At the same time, they participated in political movements. However, where the solemn Marxists were marching on the front lines of the barricades, the situationists arranged their own masterstrokes which were targeted at the consumer-oriented lifestyle. They would dress like Santa Clauses en masse, walk into department stores and dispense free Christmas gifts to children from the shelves. The police, who were inevitably called in, then had the deplorable task of explaining to the children why they had to give up the gifts presented to them by Santa himself.

The legacy of the avant-garde in the beginning of the 20th century was just as important to the situationists as the theoretical and political dimensions of Marxism. One aim of the avant-garde was to break the boundaries of the institution of art and make art a part of life. For instance, the theatre of Antonin Artaud manifested this by not limiting drama to mere performance for an anonymous audience. Theatre was to penetrate life itself and become an intrinsic part of it, in addition to society and other cultural forms (Bürger 1984). It had to step over the proscenium that separated the stage and the audience. Situationists also wanted to revolutionize the everyday by relying on the creative force of imagination, in which humor and gaiety played no small role. They wanted to give the kiss of life to theory and join it with the pleasure brought by artistic activities. The situationists operated in several European countries, but the core of the movement was small and only consisted of a few dozen people (cf. Plant 1992).

A dictionary defines spectacle as a grand but shallow play, film, festivity or event. Thus, it is something contrived and ludicrous. However, the spectacle has its roots in the history of optical devices. Perhaps the most important of which is the *laterna magica*, invented already in the 17th century, which could reflect images to entertain crowds. Erkki Huhtamo, a researcher in visual culture, describes (1997, 14) the *laterna magica*:

> With *laterna magica* it is possible to show a picture that is otherwise only good for being admired by one viewer to a whole crowd of people. Hence, the vicissitude of *laterna magica* articulates into the history of spectacles, 'addressing' people with the means of audio-visual technologies and the gradual change of crowds into audiences. From the perspective of the archaeology of the moving picture, the feature film is only one, rather a late phase in this development.

The Debordian spectacle includes these kinds of meanings, but it is also much more than that: a spectacle is a functional relationship constructed between people where pictures have a central position. "The Spectacle is not a collection of images, but a social relation among people, mediated by images", Debord (1987, chap. 4) writes. What can this mean?

If Debord is now expected to give a clear definition of spectacle, he will let us down. Debord churns out contradictions, metaphors and aphorisms, and compresses lots of stuff in short sentences. *Society of the Spectacle* does not provide an actual scheme of clear structure, but consists of numbered paragraphs or chapters. Here I focus on certain characterizations of the spectacle and read them from the viewpoint of the visual. The visual is not the only sensory dimension with regard to the effects of the spectacle, but it is certainly the most important one.

Debord (*ibid.*, chap. 18) writes:

> Where the real world changes into simple images, the simple images become real beings and effective motivations of hypnotic behavior. The spectacle, as a tendency to make one see the world by means of various specialized mediations (it can no longer be grasped directly), naturally finds vision to be the privileged human sense which the sense of touch was for other epochs; the most abstract, the most mystifiable sense corresponds to the generalized abstraction of present-day society. But the spectacle is not identifiable with mere gazing, even combined with hearing. It is that which escapes the activity of men, that which escapes reconsideration and correction by their work. It is the opposite of dialogue. Wherever there is independent representation, the spectacle reconstitutes itself.

Plato's distrust of visual reality lives on in Debord's thinking. Yet, simultaneously, pictures are extremely significant because they encompass false knowledge. The world has changed into "simple images" which have become "real beings" and "motivations for hypnotic behavior". Reality has turned into a *laterna magica* of sorts. However, according to Debord it is possible to see through a spectacle by the means of the capacity to think. Evidently he was planning his own philosophy to become the foundation to this critical capacity. In Plato's thinking, the idea of the good and true knowledge were connected: acquiring correct knowledge enables the realization of the good and hence opens the route to a just society, whereas relying on assumptions or false knowledge fetters the realization of the good. It is possible to trace elements of the same idea in Debord's ideas where the recognition of the fallacy of the spectacle at least gives access to the *opportunity* to a real life.

Juxtaposing Plato and Debord is an inherently dangerous endeavor because they are separated by approximately 2500 years in the history of Western thinking. Debord's text was published a quarter of a century after World War II, in the late 1960s. The economic growth of the postwar years had helped European societies to their feet, increasing consumption, and, consequently, the increase of pictorial advertising was explosive. In this situation, the aesthetic form of objects and the visual order connected to it were more obvious than ever before. Debord paints a portrait of a society which believed it could provide its members with whatever they wanted as well as satisfy all their needs and dreams. However, the all-encompassing satisfaction of needs only seemed possible by consuming more and more goods. Consuming, in turn, is an activity which, according to the situationists, can not fulfill people's true needs. A new commodity pleases for a while but leaves behind an even greater sense of dysphoria. This makes the object form itself a way of being and meaning of life for people. Objects become crystallized in the Spectacle which is "capital to such a degree of accumulation that it becomes an image" (*ibid.*, chap. 34). People are alienated because they believe they are what the spectacle offers to them.

Alienation can be controversial, though. Why assume in the first place that there is some pure and original experience from which people alienate themselves through false consumption? Why can't consuming, or identifying with the spectacle, be a conscious game? Here we find ourselves amidst the most fundamental questions of subjectivity. How free is consuming actually? How do advertisements unconsciously affect our desire to purchase a new thing? How, in the first place, can we consciously control our lives in front of the enchantment of things?

The thought of Debord and the situationists still thrives within the consumerism-critical movement. One example is the Canadian Media Foundation, whose best known campaign internationally is probably the "Buy Nothing Day". The foundation also publishes *Adbusters* magazine, which focuses not only on dissecting the operations of brand names and multinational corporations but also on parodying *Nike*, *McDonalds*, *Coca-Cola* and other brands. The magazine's subtitle *Journal of Mental Environment* says it all. In short, the goal is to cleanse "the mental environment" of the alienated filth of advertisements and brands, to free consumers from the yoke of the Spectacle and to make them human beings again. Hence the magazine wages guerrilla war against the visual orders crystallized in established brands. Part of the arsenal includes anti-advertisements (see Fig 1.1, p.2), which are produced in top studios to be as cutting edge as the counterparts they parody.

Consumers thus participate in the social orders of society along with objects and the visual orders formed by their pictorial quality (Spectacle). This is precisely the question in Debord's (*ibid.*) remark that "the spectacle is not a collection of images, but a social relation among people, mediated by images." Hence, the pictorial and visual are not merely pictorial and visual but linked in many ways to consuming and people's socialization as part of the social order.

Debord does not venture into how alienation takes place. The answer to this could be sought by contemplating the seductive quality of the spectacle. People are willing to invest their own desires in it and see the possibility to be something they are not. The imagery of the spectacle can give a promise of youth, beauty, power or masculinity.

Psychoanalytically thinking, then, the core is identification with an ideal ego; for instance, the visual orders provided by traditional masculinity: it is usually easier to identify oneself with an ideal masculine body than with a scrawny guy. Psychoanalytically it can also be understood why the spectacle is incapable of redeeming the promises it gives. A human being can never reach his or her ideal self, because—true to its name—it is an *ideal*; a state of desire and wish but never accessible within real existence. The spectacle therefore makes a person reach out to something he is not, but something that the tension between his ideal self and true self entice him to be. This is the road to self-alienation.

> The alienation of the spectator to the profit of the contemplated object (which is the result of his own unconscious activity) is expressed in the following way: the more he contemplates the less he lives; the more he accepts recognizing himself in the dominant images of need, the less he understands his own existence and his own desires. The externality of the spectacle in relation to the active man appears in the fact that his own gestures are no longer his but those of another who represents them to him. This is why the spectator feels at home nowhere, because the spectacle is everywhere. (*Ibid.*, chap. 30)

Debord's spectacle is therefore an *evil imagery*. It is also an omnipotent imagery, which along with objectification continuously gains ground in yet new domains of society and interaction. In capitalistic society a structural coercion prevails to produce ever more new things which are then visualized as part of the media imagery, a gallery where consumers pick up building material for their own identities to fill the gap between the real and the desired state of being. Consuming things and images links together economic and symbolic cycles which guarantee social continuity. An image is visualized economy.

Debord himself still believed at the end of the 1960s that the spectacle can be averted. Naturally, it is paramount to understand how the spectacle works. Only then it is possible to utilize the strategy which Debord describes through the concept of *détournement*. The term can be translated as either hijacking meaning or leading astray. As an example of *détournement* Sadie Plant uses the adapted cartoons published in the magazine *Internationale Situationniste*, in which real love stories were infiltrated with balloons of political propaganda (Plant 1992, 86–87). To simplify slightly, détournement is a way of shaking up meanings through their own tools: the seductive is made ludicrous, the solemn hilarious, the ideal caricature-like. It is precisely this strategy that underscores the previously mentioned Media Foundation: to caricature brand advertising through its own means.

According to Plant (*ibid.*, 75), the situationists were of the opinion, nonetheless, that it is not possible to position oneself outside the spectacle. Every form of critique targeted at the spectacle can itself become the spectacle. The teachings of the historical avant-garde were well-received: anti-art becomes art, and in fact reinforces the institution of art against which it was originally aimed. To make an analogy: a revolutionary speech act becomes part of advertising because every new product is revolutionary. Even though the situationists understood the spectacle as a visual order which inevitably spreads out into all areas of life, *détournement* provided at least some sort of a tool of resistance. This kind of hope is no longer to be found in Jean Baudrillard's 'ecstasy of communication', in which the spectacle has become simulation.

Baudrillard's Endless Simulation

> We no longer partake of the drama of alienation, but are in the ecstasy of communica-
> tion. And this ecstasy is obscene. Obscene is that which eliminates the gaze, the image
> and every representation. Obscenity is not confined to sexuality, because today there is a
> pornography of information and communication, a pornography of circuits and networks,
> of functions and objects in their legibility, availability, regulation, forced signification,
> capacity to perform, connection, polyvalence, their free expression... It is no longer the ob-
> scenity of the hidden, the repressed, the obscure, but that of the visible, the all-too-visible,
> the more-visible-than-visible; it is the obscenity of that which no longer contains a secret
> and is entirely soluble in information and communication. (Baudrillard 1988a, 22)

It takes a patient mind to dissect Baudrillard's notions and find out what he is actually driving at. When speaking about the pictorial and visual, he is neverthe-less hard to overlook, because his theories of simulation and the hyper-real have received extraordinarily wide attention even outside philosophy and social scien-tific discourse. Baudrillard can be read in at least two different ways. One can read his texts as if they were serious attempts to achieve something essential about this age of communication networks, digital interfaces and visual orders. On the other hand, they can be understood as games that do not even try to say anything all that important about anything.

Baudrillard's writing career began as such in the 1960s, when he published his first book, *Le système des objets* (1966). During the next decade he discussed the consumer society in his writings, Marx's economic critique, systems of signs and fashion. Up until Baudrillard wrote *L'échance symbolique et la mort* (1976) he moved within traditional sociological discourse. After this, however, his literary style and analyses went wild and took a different course from the parameters of scientific writing. In the quote above from his work *The Ecstasy of Communication*, Baudrillard characterizes all social meanings as having become transparent and simultaneously, having been taken to the extreme. Nothing is obscene any longer, for all is transparent. Nothing can be revealed, for all is already exposed. Where Plato believed that images were false, mere imperfect reflections of the world of ideas, Baudrillard thinks that there is nothing behind images. Only a visual surface exists on which images, texts and streams of binary digits unite and separate in their continuous play of partings.

Baudrillard knew Debord in the 1960s and there are common features to be found in the writings of these two theoreticians. Baudrillard's playful and exaggerated style resembles formulations of the *Society of the Spectacle*. Whereas Debord still seemed to believe in the human capacity to sink into the false world of advertising and thereby lose the opportunity for real life, Baudrillard was certain that the pureness of life lay expressly in its synthetic and mendacious quality. The meretricious is more real than the real. Ecstatic communication, devouring images and information, has broken through the opposition between the real and the alienated selves. Visual orders created by the media are their own reality, which does not reflect any primary reality. Representation has disappeared and visual culture is precisely as material as the visual orders formed around us by objects. Pornography is a metaphor for extreme visuality.

Is this so?

Apparently, Baudrillard's theorizing is not meant to be descriptive of reality—after all, isn't representation dead? Theory, therefore, is part of the system it analyzes. Baudrillard's style also has an ethical dimension: his texts function as a critique of social science that forever strives to be dry, no-nonsense truth. This agenda is formulated as follows:

> It is not enough for theory to describe and analyse, it must itself be an event in the universe it describes. In order to do this theory must partake of and become the acceleration of this logic. It must tear itself from all referents and take pride only in the future. (…) Theory is, at any rate, destined to be diverted, deviated, and manipulated. It would be better for theory to divert itself, than to be diverted from itself. If it aspires to any *effets de vérité* it must eclipse them through its own movement (Baudrillard 1988a, 99–100).

Hence, in the era of simulation and hyper-real reality can no longer be discerned from its image. For instance, we can no longer say which natural world is more real for us: the mountain brook streaming in a beer ad or the mountain brook in the Northern wilderness. If I have never been to the mountains, the nature photograph of an advertisement is certainly a more real Lappish wilderness to me than the actual, existing wilderness. It can even replace it. To take another example: in a commercial for a holiday in the Mediterranean I see a turquoise sea and a half-empty sandy beach. For months I can lie under that sun in a blissful fantasy, until I finally get to—if I do—visit the actual holiday resort in reality. It may be that the beaches are crowded and the waters murky, but I can nevertheless keep on fantasizing and hope that the next time round the reality corresponds with the image in the commercial. In a sense, then, the reality of the image is much more real than going to the place itself. But how did we get to this point?

Debord believed that what occurs in the background of the spectacle are the production of goods, consumption and the social relations built on them; namely, traditional capitalism. Baudrillard, in his turn, claims that in the era of simulation the production of meanings is no longer tied in any way to the production of material objects, things. In a sense, capitalism no longer exists. He sees only arbitrary combinations of different brands and images, in which new differences are continuously born without any reference to the external reality of the brand. When people consume brands by buying branded products they do not hide their real nature or real needs, because their psyche is nothing other than perpetual connections, separations and reconnections of these brands. This naturally does not mean that the sense or concept of alienation does not exist; they simply are not any more meaningful than other feelings. Even the sense of reality is a result of the impact of simulation.

Baudrillard has constructed a historical model through which he explains the birth of the society of simulation. He (1998b, 135–148) separates three different eras, simulacrums[5], in each of which the status of the sign has been different. The first era he calls the era of mimesis. It began with the Renaissance when the feudal social system began to crumble away. In feudal society, people were fixed to their social positions and mobility was nearly non-existent. Also visual signs were stable: one's clothing immediately gave away which social class (caste) the person belonged to. Signs were closely connected to social status. These kinds of societies were cruel and there was no playing around with signs. Moreover, the number of signs was very limited and they were not arbitrary.

Baudrillard (*ibid.*, 136) writes:"The arbitrary nature of the sign arises when, instead of linking two people in unbreachable reciprocity, the sign begins, in signifying, to refer to the disenchanted universe of the signified—the common denominator of the real world, to which nobody really has any further obligation."

Baudrillard raises fashion as one indicator of the radical change that took place during the Renaissance. Meanings linked to clothing were no longer so very tightly bound to the social status of the people who wore them. Hence, along with the Renaissance, the sign is relieved of its immediate social bond, which also makes fraud and imitation possible. It is possible for people to disguise themselves—at least in principle, to pretend they are something they are not. In a modern sense, the sign was then born during the Renaissance because it was then that the question of the correlation between a sign and the reality became topical.

However, it was the birth of industrial mass production that revolutionized the world of signs. This era Baudrillard calls *industrial simulacrum*. The mass production of goods pushed the economy of brands into motion because it produced an incredible number of signs and things. There was no longer any sense in inquiring about the origin of signs or things because the origin lay in the production itself. Of goods that were mass-produced, not one was more real or natural than the rest. Mass production also introduced the principle of series in the domain of the production of meanings, which in turn wrecked the reference relation of the brand for good. "In the series, objects are transformed indefinitely into simulacra of one another and, with objects, so are the people who produce them. Only the extinction of the original reference permits the generalized law of equivalence, which is to say, the *very possibility of production*" (*ibid.*, 137).

Whereas naturalness was the fundamental principle of the first simulacrum, human work and material production were that for the era of serial production. Through them, also the production of meaning becomes possible. From Baudrillard's viewpoint Debord's *Society of the Spectacle* is still a prisoner of this phase of industrial simulacrum. For Debord, objects, capital and production are the central dynamics of the society of spectacle. According to Baudrillard, the hard core of the serial production of goods lies not, however, in production or objects but in the idea of serialism itself and in the notion that it is possible to make innumerable amounts of copies of any object. The industrial revolution is thus semiotic; a revolution of social sign systems which blazed the way to simulation and the end of capitalism.

In the simulacrum of the third phase, the simulation described above or the era of the *metaphysics of code* has finally been reached. There signs merge with each other without any relation to production, origin or nature.

Thus, the systems of the production of social meaning move from the era of disciplined signs (class society) through serial signs and production (industrial society) to the collapse of the sign and its transformation into reality itself (the society of simulation, hyper-real). Particularly in the last phase pictorial quality is an essential resource, because the central semiotic working mechanism of the hyperreal society is actualized in it: an image as reality.[6]

Baudrillard takes wild leaps from era to era and detects symptoms of simulation already in connection with the iconoclastic altercations in the 8th and 9th centuries. At that time, the argument was about whether pictures of God can be made in the first place. The iconoclasts, the razers of images, argued their standpoint on the basis of the prohibitions of the Old Testament, the cheap materials of the icons, and with the notion that imaging God limits His sacrosanct essence. According to Baudrillard, the iconoclasts in fact feared that icons would replace the pure idea of God reachable by thought. An image of God raises the question: what if there is nothing but the image? What if God is nothing but his image? If the iconoclasts had merely believed that images obscure the real Godliness, they would have had no reason to drag them down. "But their metaphysical despair came from the idea that the images concealed nothing at all, and that in fact they were not images, such as the original model would have made them, but actually perfect simulacra forever radiant with their own fascination. But this death of the divine referential has to be exorcised at all cost."(Baudrillard, 1983, 8–9)

Baudrillard therefore sees elements of simulation already in the early Middle Ages, which naturally justifies the question: Is simulation really a principle of production tied to our time only, as Baudrillard leads us to believe on the other hand? Here our philosopher is hopelessly contradictory but certainly right when he notes: This "millennial quarrel is still with us today" (*ibid.*, 8).

Let us think about the much discussed *Ecce Homo* photographs of Swedish photographer Elisabeth Ohlson. (Fig. 2.7) The photographs depict Jesus hanging

Figure 2.7 *Swedish photographer Elisabeth Ohlson's photograph from the series Ecce Homo Matthew 26:26–28.* © Copyright Elisabeth Ohlson.

out with prostitutes, transvestites and homosexuals. The photographer herself argues for her topic by reminding us that Jesus always took a stand for minorities and those discriminated against. Many members of the parliament, clergymen and private citizens, however, demanded the pictures be banned because in their interpretation they did not represent the real Christ. To follow Baudrillard's notion, we could ask whether these razers of images were worried about the pictures distorting the concept of Christian divinity, or that the pictures actually showed that there is no final truth about God in the first place. Did the photographs unveil the liability of the faith of the outraged?

The fundamental question is of representation. Baudrillard believes—as was already established earlier—that the era of simulation has discarded representation. Representation "starts from the principle that the sign and the real are equivalent (even if this equivalence is utopian, it is a fundamental axiom). Conversely, simulation starts from the *utopia* of this principle of equivalence, *from the radical negation of the sign as value*, from the sign as reversion and death sentence of every reference. Whereas representation tries to absorb simulation by interpreting it as false representation, simulation envelops the whole edifice of representation as itself a simulacrum" (Baudrillard 1983, 11).

For an image, four ways of being open up all of which in the end return to simulation (Baudrillard 1988b, 170).

Firstly, an image can reflect the innermost reality. At the first glance, this situation is the most general and uncomplicated. The standpoint could perhaps be characterized as naively realistic: an image represents the reality external to it at least with relative accuracy. We can also talk about photographic reality.

Secondly, an image can mask and distort the innermost reality. This is a criticism and denial of the first standpoint, but merges with it seamlessly. In both cases an image is assessed in its relation to the reality it represents, that is, an image is a clear representation. If we think of the discourse concerning the truthfulness of a photograph, it most commonly moves on these two axes. The question is: in what way a photograph either corresponds or does not correspond to reality. The critique Ohlson's photographs faced functioned most often in this dimension.

The third possible relation of an image with reality is that it obscures the fact that there is no such thing as innermost reality. In this, the functions of an image and the visual have already departed from simple representation and have begun a life of their own. The visual becomes an object of perception as an independent system, and one of its characteristics is—through its reality effects—to remove the question of reality per se out of the agenda.

The fourth form of the visual embodies the notion that an image no longer bears any relation at all to any reality; it is its own simulacrum. This fourth dimension of an image quite closely skirts the third.

An image can hence:

- be a reflection of a basic reality.
- mask and pervert basic reality.
- mask the absence of basic reality.
- bear no relation to any reality and be its own simulacrum.

These four ways of being visual position themselves in a historical order, in which the first phases precede the era of simulation. However, it is self-evident that the truthfulness of pictures is still a subject for debate in the sense how well they represent reality. As I see it, Baudrillard indeed drives at the notion that the earlier ways of setting the problems of picture and reality are still alive and well, but they arise expressly from the functioning of simulation. Simulation continuously re-suscitates earlier notions of the visual. This creates nostalgia for the past to which we can never again return.

Baudrillard uses Debord's notion of the spectacle for his own cynical purposes. Visual orders only exist as superficial sign games. When reading Baudrillard, there is reason to keep in mind that his nihilism is targeted at traditional social scientific theorizing. Perhaps it is precisely here where philosopher Friedrich Nietzsche's (1844–1900) influence becomes most apparent. Like Nietzsche, Baudrillard relieves science from the burden of seeking the truth and begins to actualize a kind of here-and-now ethics, in which writing itself becomes a weapon against academic truths.

There is seductive power in Debord's and Baudrillard's theories, as in all strong and total constructions of thought. Debord's idea of the spectacle which alienates people from their true being is, however, one-dimensional. Despite this he reaches something essential in the relations between consumption, the visual and identity. Exorbitant commitment to the spectacle as the source of one's own identity may be 'fun', but just as well it can contain feelings of emptiness and promises that will never come true. I myself think like Debord; it is useless to seek identity from the shelves of a store, and it is most unfortunate if the self-image relies on an advertisement image.

Baudrillard, on his part, is so hardened by simulation that he does not bother himself with childish questions of the agency of a human subject. Yet, both theo-reticians are so enamored with their own abstractions that they forget to take a look at the world surrounding them.

To end this chapter, I outline a few everyday ways of visual production, which can at their best challenge the existing visual orders and that way assist people to be in better control over their own lives.

AGAINST ORDERS!

People do not merely adapt to visual orders but actively construct them. They decorate their homes, alter their appearance, and tune up the looks of their kids and dogs.

Buying a pair of eyeglasses is a good example of how seeing and being seen are entangled (a topic I return to in more detail in the next chapter). The obvious function of eyeglasses is, after all, to help people see better. However, when I browse through the frame selections at an optician's, the thought begins to creep to mind that correcting the way one is seen is precisely as important as correcting the way one sees. Many people have experienced how painful a task it really is to find a suitable pair of frames in comparison to the simple, scientific determining of the correct strength and quality of the lenses themselves. I see better when I wear glasses, but by choosing the right frames I am also seen better and I can position myself as a part of a certain world of meanings and visual order.

One summer—just to show off—I got myself a pair of sunglasses with yellow-tinted lenses and thick, black frames. Once, driving by an outdoor café, someone yelled after me: "Hey, look, it's Mika Häkkinen". When I went to the beach to hang out with my friends, one of them jibed: "Cool Jimi Tenor glasses". The first wiseacre saw the yellow lenses which are the summer trademark of Formula 1 driver Mika Häkkinen; the other noticed the frames and immediately linked me with the imagery of 'brainy' rock'n'roll. I indeed achieved my narcissistic goal: my glasses did draw attention, and through them I was coded as part of visual orders to which I most certainly do not feel I belong.

Now, more than ever before in its history, humankind is *producing the pictorial*. Family albums, home videos, computer user interfaces are all means to construct personal visual orders. The spread of music videos through MTV and other similar TV channels has encouraged many garage bands to make their own videos. In Finland there are also thousands of bands which have attempted to construct their own visual countenance with their own homemade videos. Meanwhile, a field of learning through experiments, imitations and trial and error has been created. The rudimentary dramaturgy of visual expression is learned the hard way. An even broader swath of private video making has opened up along with the introduction of high-quality, lightweight and relatively inexpensive video cameras on the market. Other practices of producing the pictorial are easy to name: nature photography, constructing home web pages, drawing and painting.

The photograph has been a central form of self-representation throughout the 20th century. Diaries are written by few but a camera is found in almost in every home. Mostly people photograph life's turning points or events that diverge from the everyday: weddings, graduations, baptisms and holiday trips. Few families have albums that contain domestic rows captured on film, or making breakfast or even reading the kids a bedtime story. Looking at family albums is a social rite as people spend time together through the means of looking at and explaining photographs. Most of the time people construct their albums subordinate to the potential gaze of guests. In other words, only certain pictures are selected to be shown that can be shared with others. Hence a family album becomes an exhibition of the family for the miniature public formed by the close circle of friends and relatives with whom it is shared. Through the means of album photos, it is possible to journey to another place and time. They help to remember, arouse images and associations and provide a comparison point to the present moment. Photos are material objects and visual representations which have grown to be part of one's personal history. I once asked a friend which object he would rescue first in case of fire. He answered without hesitation: my photos.

In his article *Domestic Photography and Digital Culture* British visual culture researcher Don Slater (1995a) discusses the place of family photos in digitalized culture. According to Slater, the picture production of families is linked with two broader, intertwined phenomena; namely, consuming and free time. Photography is consumption of photographic technology—most often during people's free time which itself becomes a subject of pictorial representation. Photography entered the domain of consumption actually only at the end of the 19th century when Kodak introduced its first user-friendly, lightweight camera, and began to market it with the well-known slogan "You Press the Button, We Do the Rest." The photographer was released from the laborious process of developing the pictures. This created the preconditions for an enormous private picture production and made photography a popular hobby. Moreover, the new technology was genderized from the very beginning: the simplicity of the technique became a hook which was used to market cameras for women as early as the beginning of the 20th century (Holland 1997, 129). The union between consuming camera technology and free time is even clearer if we think about, for instance, nature photography. It is easy to invest enormous amounts of money in optical systems, tripods and cameras themselves. There are only a handful of professional nature photographers in Finland, but as a leisure time activity it is extremely popular.

Slater (1995a, 134) writes:"We construct ourselves *for* the image and *through* images."

I remember an event from my own childhood when the whole family went to a studio to be immortalized—an illustrative expression in itself. The conditions for this studio photograph were rather unexceptional. The family had just reunited after my parents briefly separated. All four of us, father, mother, little sister and I, were carefully dressed up. Father was positioned on my mother's right side, I stood in front of my father on a slightly lower stand and my little sister was given a similar position in front of my mother. Everyone looked directly, openly, and straight into the camera. We were reconstructing our family identity and, at the same time, our individual identities as members of the family. Things were right again. The order of the photograph (from the reading direction of the picture father was first; standing tallest because of his height; and us children at our parent's feet in the correct order in terms of gender) positioned the members of our family in the roles of the nuclear family. Thus, the visual order of the family photograph is a social order. During all of the remaining years our family stayed together as such, the photo looked upon us from the mantelpiece as a symbolic confirmation of family harmony and happiness.

Slater (*ibid.*, 138–139) indeed remarks

> Family photography is not documentary in aim or attitude: it is sentimental because it attempts to fix transcendent and tender emotions and identifications on people and moments hauled out of ordinary time and mundanity, the better to foreground an idealised sense of their value, and the value of our relationship to them, in the present and in memory (…) the idealisation is indeed conventional, achieved not through the specificity of the relationship but the social acceptability of certain representational conventions for depicting these values: domestic photographs are closely determined by their *genres*.

In this connection, genre refers to the ways of production of photographs and posing for them in the family circles. Graduation photos, wedding pictures and birthday documentaries complete with candle blowing that are stored away in the albums of different families are, after all, very similar to each other.

The family album can in fact be understood as a broader whole than a mere book of photographs. Its sphere includes portraits of family members or other relatives that are placed on the bookcase or hung on walls; small-sized pictures to be carried in a wallet; digital snapshots packed on a CD–ROM. If the band posters found in the rooms of teenagers and other such pictorial representations are added in, the family album expands further. These pictures also participate in the processing of the family members' identities in many ways. Firstly, they can function as identification surfaces of youngsters: the stars in the picture are identified with in one way or another. Secondly, these pictures and the visual order constructed through them mark the youngster's own territory. He or she has been given permission to construct the room to reflect him or herself. Thirdly, pictures in themselves are goods to be consumed; they are music transformed into pictures that live on as images along with the auditory sensation or even without it.

Television, computer games and the Internet connect family members to eternally new and more numerous overlapping pictorial and visual orders. In fact, Slater thinks that the family album will soon cease to have such a central role in the process of constructing identities. He refers to certain market reports which indicate that people still (in the mid-1990s) value their family albums. According to these reports, 39% of people consider the family album their most valuable possession. However, the report also revealed that these very same respondents flip through their albums very rarely. 60% of the respondents and their families looked at the albums not more often than once a year or less, and 79% only once in six months or less often. The family album is highly esteemed but seldom used (*ibid.*, 138–139).

Slater assumes that the more often the pictures are looked at, the stronger the album functions as a tool for constructing identity. However, we can assume just as well that it is expressly the awareness of the existence of the photographs and their high esteem that reveal their central role in terms of identity, despite the fact that they are not very often looked at. Naturally Slater's finding does not apply to pictures than hang on walls or stand on surfaces. They are a permanent part of the home's visual order; they have a solid place in this order similar to the people they portray which have a solid place in the social network of the family. In fact, through photographs, dead relatives or family members continue to be seen or even alive, in a sense. However, this does not undermine Slater's assumption according to which the role of the family album has decreased due to the invasion of digital visual culture. The family album remains important, but it has new visual rivals as tools for the identity construction process of the family and its members.

Of course, the most abundant flood of images gushes from the television. Computer games, with the visual, auditory and textual pleasure they provide, have become the strongest rival of television. A watcher, player or user—whatever term is preferred—can make choices by choosing different TV channels, renting videos and DVDs, and clicking the icons or menus on the computer screen. However, in each case the spectator ends up facing a visual order designed in advance: there is a limited amount of channels; in computer games there are only that many options. Slater (*ibid.*, 141) crystallizes the idea: "The programmer tries to foresee possible and desirable events that could take place, offers a structured way of making a choice between a limited number of foreseeable events, then tries to programme in the consequences of any of these choices, with further choices down the line. If flow can be represented by the television channel, the decision pathway is best represented by the 'menu' in a computer programme."

The essential in menus is the fact that they are pre-determined and easily consumed "structures of time and activity". They create a paradox: a *passive choice* between a certain amount of closed options. Slater (*ibid.*, 143) remarks: "Freedom to manoeuvre within, as well as to choose between, these structures is no substitute for the power to create structures."

However, this does not mean that people would not be active as they for instance play games or surf between TV channels, but

> We might have extremely creative and rewarding involvements with the image activities which make up leisure time; the point is simply that personal images of ourselves do not seem to find a place there. We might see this by contrast with the use of digital technology in music: new music technologies stimulate new forms of self-expression in ways which image technology does not. Rap, sampling, even karaoke or the simple process of putting together a party tape make for interesting contrasts to putting together a family album. (*Ibid.*, 142)

What does Slater mean by "personal images of ourselves"? Are not family albums precisely full of those? In Slater's opinion, photographs and practices of producing pictures in family circles, however, are limited. Even though people photograph and videotape a lot, they seldom use the pictures for a *conscious* construction, exploration or questioning of their identities. A mass-scale picture production is born, which, through its visual order, contributes to the upholding of traditional family forms and gender roles, as well as power structures connected to them. In order to understand Slater's notion there is reason to keep in mind that he has tight bonds to the traditions of British production of culture and different practices of critical photography, where people have attempted to investigate and mould their surroundings and their own identities through photographs. The question is that of the ethics of making pictures: we must strive to understand in what way, for instance, family photos maintain intra-family gendered practices or, say, the myth of the nuclear family. What this understanding can lead to is that a prevailing visual order is not merely repeated, but people try to create imagery and ways of representation that are *genuinely their own*.

The critical practices of picture making that Slater refers to can be found by the dozens. For instance, in the 1970s a community photography movement was born in the British Isles, whose members attempted to produce visual representations about their own living environment through the means of photographs and videos. People were encouraged to photograph themselves and each other in such a way that they simultaneously analyzed the visual orders of their habitat, as well as the social and political meanings connected to them. The *Bootle Art in Action* group was born in the circles of the movement. Its members photographed themselves as part of their decayed, nearly slum-like living environment in Liverpool. As a result of the project, a book *Bootle—A Pictorial Study of Dockland Community* was published. One of the central objectives of the activities was to inform decision-makers about what kind of an environment the children of the book-makers had to grow up in. The residents also wanted to create a feasible option to public picture production, the visual order of which had neither room nor place for photographs taken on the residents' own terms. In some aspects, the aspirations of the group resemble the ideas of the so-called citizen journalism of the 1990s. One of the points of departure of so-called citizen journalism was to encourage people to make journalism themselves about issues they find important. Hence, photography in the Docklands was closely connected to people's own volition to construct the pictorial order of their own area themselves.[7]

Bootle Art in Action is only one example of the widespread self-determined picture production that was prevalent at the end of the 1960s and 1970s.[8] A more popular means than the traditional photographic camera was the video camera, which has continuously developed to be lighter, cheaper and of higher technical quality. A video camera is loaded with great expectations because as a medium it is equivalent to television, which is usually part of business activities of large corporations or the public service sector. Through the means of the video, people have striven to create their own publicity next to great publicities. Thus, starting from the 1970s, alternative movements and different social minorities have produced videos from their own points of departure. Numerous alternative visual agencies have also been created in the developing countries.

In his book *Cultures of Vision* (1995) visual culture researcher Ron Burnett describes experiments led by French Fred Forest, in which residents of a nursing home were encouraged to videotape their environment. In this connection, Forest listed seven goals he considered important in his experiment (see Burnett 1995, 82):

- to dynamize human relations in the community through the use of video;
- to study how the seniors (who were all former construction workers) react to video and in general to the arrival of new instruments of communication;

- to allow the community to learn from its perceptions of its own activities;
- to modify the relationship between individuals and the group;
- to stimulate exchanges between individuals and the group;
- to liberate the creativity and imagination of the seniors;
- to allow them to give expression to their latent, unrealized needs.

Burnett does not tell how well the experiment succeeded. Instead, he claims that the seven points Forest lists reflect more extensively the objectives of self-determined or community-based video production of the 1970s and 1980s. The field is too extensive to go into in this connection, but what is essential is that the objective of these movements has been to strive for self-determined visual production and therefore to produce pictures, even learn from the process of making pictures. The goal has been to become detached from consuming pictures and move towards producing them.

In Finland as well visual representations have been produced whose goal is to bring the experiences of the private or the local into wider discussion. The question is one of challenging the prevailing visual order, or even creating an open conflict through visual means such as in the following example which brings this chapter to the end.

The story proceeds as follows:

The Vuores area is a green zone of woods and lakes in the borderland between the city of Tampere and the neighboring Lempäälä municipality. The area is quiet; penetrated only by a few roads along which there is a small village and a few other scattered houses. The houses include an old estate, the Annisto manor, where photographer Juha Suonpää, his wife Marja-Leena Korte-Suonpää and their two little sons live. On one spring morning the Suonpääs read a news article in the country's largest daily paper according to which the entire Vuores area was going to be turned into a housing development for 10,000–15,000 people. A shopping center was planned to be built on the exact spot where their home stood. The Suonpääs were shocked both by the plan itself and the way they came to learn about it. They began to fight for their home by organizing public events, writing to newspapers, making complaints about the procedure and conduct of authorities, and by producing their own imagery about the impact of the project on the life of their family.

Suonpää wrote an opinion piece in the local paper *Aamulehti* (20.1.1999), in which he clarified his views about what was happening. He constructed a picture with a photo manipulation program to accompany the column which showed lumbering concrete blocks of flats stooping over the Annisto manor. (Fig. 2.8)

Figure 2.8 Juha Suonpää's digital photo collage of the Vuores neighborhood planned for Tampere. The photo was published in the regional daily newspaper Aamulehti 20.1.1999. © Copyright Juha Suonpää.

The picture was captioned: "View of the Future? Is this what the Vuores district around the Annisto manor landscape looks like in a few years? Authority-centered town planning—a shock to a local resident." "Computer picture by Juha Suonpää", was mentioned at the bottom of the picture. A few weeks later (7.2.) the same photo manipulation popped up in the TV talk show *Palaneen Käry*, where Suonpää was also invited. Deputy city manager Lasse Eskonen lifted an enlargement of the photo in front of the cameras and said: "New homes are going to be built much further than what this defective picture, that Suonpää published in *Aamulehti*, shows. This kind of illustration is called lying." (Here, I refrain from commenting on whether Suonpää's photo corresponds or does not correspond with the reality of Vuores. As I am writing this, the projects have not even been started.)

When housing estates are planned, the town planning authorities construct and reconstruct different alternatives, draw maps and sketches. At some point, a potential scale model is commissioned from an architectural agency, which gives an aerial perspective to what the area would look like when built. (In fact, no one ever looks at the place from this perspective in the future.) With current technology it is even possible to construct 3-D digital spaces in which the positioning of the buildings can be perceived from several different angles. Somewhere along the process these pictures are then disseminated to the public on the pages of newspapers as representations of what the area will look like after being built. Mostly, these pictures are made from the viewpoint of the decision-makers, builder and/or architectural agency. Suonpää went and broke the rules of the game in advance by publicizing a photo manipulation made from the viewpoint of a person whose immediate living environment would change as a consequence of the building project. The traditional visual monopoly of the constructors was broken.

The situation thus created raised the issue of the power relations linked to a visual order and its creation. *Who has the opportunity to represent plans that have a fundamental impact on, for instance, the formation of a townscape?* From what viewpoints are the visualizations made? What interests are connected to their creation? A building designed by an architectural agency can look extremely beautiful as a scale model that is made in order to sell the plan to the decision-makers. Yet, what does the building look like if perceived from a window of the house next door, when the windows no longer open to a park scene but smack dab next to the wall of the new building? A visual order is thus always an intersection of many different interests. The essential question indeed is: *Whose visual order are we talking about?*

Suonpää did not settle for simply constructing a digital picture and bringing it to the public. He bought a video camera and began to document the life of his family and the public events organized around the theme of the Vuores building plan. He succeeded in involving a national TV channel with its professional producers. A documentary called Vuores was broadcast on TV 3.2.2000 and shown at the Tampere International Film Festival during the same year. In terms of manuscript, the Vuores documentary is pathetic. It strives for nothing more than portraying the Suonpää family life in a situation where their future is under threat. Suonpää extended the imagery of an ordinary home video or family album into a public story, and thus broke the border between the private and the public—but on his own terms. He exploited publicity. The documentary also gives deputy city manager Lasse Eskonen an opportunity to make a long comment in which he remarks that Suonpää distorts every single thing about the issue. An interesting detail in the documentary is how a representative of the City of Tampere announces during a meeting that the event is being filmed "by the organizers" and requires that others not use their cameras. The question is again one of the power relations linked to visual orders: who has the right to visualize the event, whose picture material is allowed to be disseminated in public?

The birth process of the Vuores documentary and its broadcast on the national TV network raise many questions of personal picture production. By making a sufficiently professional and high-quality video, as well as marketing it every way possible, Suonpää succeeded in breaking the borderline between local and national. Through the means of the video, the viewpoint of one resident extended into national publicity. On the other hand, simply filming the whole social conflict as such created documentary material and made the decision-makers rethink the project from new perspectives. The video was significant also in the sense that it broke the borderline between the margin and the centre. The dramaturgy of the documentary made it a possession of every viewer—it was easy to identify with the story—instead of a mere personal documentary of only those initiated in the struggle. Yet, would Suonpää have succeeded in this without having a professional and impertinent grip on things from the very beginning, as well as the necessary connections to produce the video?

One problem of community video production has been the pronounced antithesis of the mainstream and the alternative. This means that programs produced and broadcast by the largest TV channels are seen as somehow bad or manipulative per se, whereas pictures produced by people themselves in the margin are liberating and critical already because of their way of production. The juxtaposition is problematic and underestimates the mainstream media as well as the interpretative capacity of the people that follow them. The mainstream and alternative are not necessarily mutually exclusive. Indeed, Suonpää's Vuores documentary is an appropriate example.

I have discussed different visual orders, and finally, the means of affecting their formation. Visual orders are powerful but not hegemonic structures to which people must adapt. People are as capable of producing their own orders as they are of adapting those provided by culture; the self-evident orders. However, I have not yet taken a look at the creation of visual orders and the essential questions in terms of functioning within them: in what way is the self of a human being or to put it in a finer way, *subjectivity* dependent on gaze and looking?

CHAPTER THREE

THE EYE, LOOKING
AND THE GAZE

A FEW YEARS AGO when I was invited to a costume party a problem instantly emerged: what role would I play? Though I entertained different ideas, I knew from the beginning what I wanted. I would attire myself in a tight-fitting Tom of Finland look: black leather, a peaked cap, and boots. Typical of me, I was slow to start arranging things. Costume rental shops were already closed, so I had to resort to Plan B: I dressed in a little black dress and accessorized it with matching pumps and a hat. I also asked a friend of mine to give me a proper makeover. After the treatment, I did look like a woman. Indeed, from a distance, I was quite a knockout.

My outfit was a success. I left the party early, though, because I had scheduled a meeting in a nearby restaurant. First I had to rush home to change. There I took one look in the mirror and it hit me: today I was not going to dress in my normal clothes, even the make-up stayed on.

The bouncer at the restaurant reacted too late. I had already entered the main dining room when he started after me. However, he realized very quickly that interfering would only make my outfit even more visible.

For the first time in my life I truly understood what it means to have heads turned. Men looked at me interested at first, but when they apprehended my true gender they jerked their eyes away from me obviously angered. Women were in better control of themselves and cast openly curious glances at me, slightly amused and clearly more merry than the men. I began to feel quite at home in my attire. I took cover behind the armor of the assumed gender and made a mental note of a paradox: the more I was looked at, the easier it was for me to hide. I savored the looks. I was in control over the situation because I realized, or at least thought I realized, what forces were at work here and what kind of a threat I posed to the identity of some of the men. I attracted looks at me and, at the same time, at other restaurant patrons near me. I could have easily caused a conflict simply by making myself available to some man—assuming that he would not have been genuinely interested or otherwise just willing to play along.

I was gripped by the experience for a few days. I had to struggle to detach myself from the mood and pleasure that the situation gave me. I learned a lot about a look, being the object of a look, and gender, which are all inseparably interconnected. At the same time, the episode was a basic course on the elasticity of sexual identity. I felt good in my costume. Was this enjoyment caused by the feeling of being in control, the looks that I was subjected to, narcissistic pleasure, the trance I experienced after crossing a gender role line, the fracturing of a masculine and heterosexual identity or perhaps all of the above? I was quite obviously encroaching on the borders of my identity, on a previously unexplored terrain. However, despite the fact that the experience was amusing, it was also demanded a lot of strenuous psychological work. By dressing up as a woman I began to understand something about the fluidity of identity and the fact that it is not possible to change identities like clothes. Gender and sexuality are linked to visible countenance, yet, they are also anchored to the unconscious and cannot be controlled in just any which way. Ultimately, they have the individual on the leash and not vice versa.

The restaurant was not particularly exclusive, but it nevertheless was the meeting place of an affluent crowd of 20- to 40-year-olds. It was clear that my costume and the identity it conveyed were blatantly discordant with the visual order of the place, where the fashion sense largely consisted of sports jackets, bright tops, jeans and medium-length skirts. Some black evening wear could be spotted here and there, usually among those on their way downstairs to a popular night club. Women were dressed as women and men like men. The ambience of the place was middle-class and heterosexual. Had I popped by the gay and lesbian bar across the street, I would have encountered a totally different visual order. Moreover, if I had an entourage tagging along with me suggesting that a stag party was under way; my outfit would have attracted attention but hardly aggression. Under my dress I would have been a man with the pleasures of the bridal bed awaiting me somewhere. I would only have reinforced the restaurant's heterosexual identity by underlining the frontier between the normal and the anomalous.

I do not imagine that my performance raised a singularly uniform reaction. Certainly there were people with diverse sexual and gender identities among the crowd. Nevertheless, I would argue that at least most of the men interpreted me as being a 'deviant.' Glances that quickly turned away were a tell-tale sign. It was as if the people were caught in the act of peeping. Probably many of the women also experienced my being as repulsive.

I noticed many people were discussing my outfit, but I myself did not speak to anyone other than my friend. Still, the air was dense with a plethora of meanings. My performance showed what an important role the looks which are directed to us play in the defining of identity. We form our conception of the environment by looking and, at the same time, wondering how we ourselves are interpreted by the looks of others and the visual orders structured on the basis of these looks. Moreover, the performance showed how strong the visual orders connected to gender really are and how little tolerance there is towards those who violate these arrangements. The visual orders in a workplace are even more binding, if we think, for example, about the dress code of a nurse, a McDonald's employee, an air hostess or a chief executive participating in business negotiations.

THE EYE IS SENSITIZED TO LIGHT

If looking and being the object of looking form such a powerful social force, there is reason to ask: *What is a look and looking?* In what way does interaction take place in a situation where verbal communication is not salient? Before contemplating the role of a look it is logical to pose a slightly more modest question: *What is an eye?* We can say, at the bare minimum, that it is a physical organ, an extraordinarily sensitive one. There are two kinds of cells in the retina, cones and rods, which react to light differently. If the wavelength of the light is sufficient, rod cells can sense it already when just a few photons reach the eye. As the intensity of the light grows, the rods stop functioning and the cone cells take over. Cones can function in light ten million times stronger than the rods. Hence, the human eye can distinguish an extremely extensive range in the strength of light.

The sense of sight does, however, have its limits. Normally we can sense only certain wavelengths of light, 400–700 nanometers, which is but a tiny sliver of the total wavelengths of electromagnetic radiation. Through technical means we can certainly extend visibility: infrared binoculars allow us to see when the wavelengths of visible light are not there.

The field of vision usually refers to the area which a human being can see without moving the eye. When a person with normal eyesight looks straight ahead, his field of vision extends 80–90 degrees from the temples and 40–50 degrees from the nose. Vertically, the field of vision spreads out to 45–50 degrees upwards and 60–80 degrees down. The fields of vision of each eye overlap in the middle. The field of vision is indeed limited and, as we all know, a human being cannot see what goes on behind his/her head. An individual looks from one point only, but is looked at from all over.

The so-called blind spot is located in the retina of each eye where the optic nerve begins. We are not aware of it because the other eye covers this area. The eye can also not focus on objects that are too close. This is the price we must pay for being able to see far. However, here again technology has extended our senses. With the aid of a space telescope we can see light years away, while with an electron microscope we can focus on the level of a single molecule. Moreover, our ability to sense the speed of motion is limited. It is not possible to perceive the flight of a bullet, but we can see a hovering eagle.

The functioning of the eye has been understood since the days of Johannes Kepler (1571–1630). However, there are still undiscovered details about how an image reflected on the retina transforms into vision. For instance, the actual workings of how we perceive two images as one stereoscopic impression and the physiology of perceiving colors remain mysteries due to the fact that we still know so very little about the functioning of the brain in general.

The sense of sight is selective, purposeful and limited. We do not register all the objects in our field of vision and the area of sharp focus is fairly narrow. When our look focuses on something, other areas in the field of vision become obscure. The physiological and biological reasons for such selectiveness can be found in evolution. In order to survive, it was imperative for a species to learn to filter essential messages from the enormous flood of stimuli in the near surroundings. Selectivity also prevents the sensory machinery from overloading.

The sense of sight is more sensitive to changes in the surroundings than the stable elements in it. The eye is keen to turn to something that moves from one place to another or changes color, brightness, form or size. Some of the most primitive species see only changes in the intensity of light and react to it by withdrawing into a hideout. One of the central tasks of the sense of sight, in biological terms, is indeed observing change in the surroundings. The art historian Rudolf Arnheim (1969, 20) notes: "To contemplate immobile parts of the surroundings is more nearly a luxury, useful at most to spot the locations of possible future changes or to view the context in which events take place." However, immobility is not the inevitable prerequisite of immutability. Even motion can be immutable, that is, predictable and safe. Animals stop reacting to constant motion if it does not present a threat to them.

The selectivity of the sense of sight can also be harmful. It can prevent us from seeing the most stable features of our living environment or to perceive a change as stable and natural. Where one person sees a destroyed river landscape, another sees a power plant generating clean energy. In a crowd we discern a familiar face much easier than an unfamiliar one: we see our superior before noticing a subordinate;

the president is ogled before his/her assistant. Eyesight thus selects its target on biological, psychological and cultural levels. Though the field of vision seems transparent, in fact it is the result of many selective processes where less is always rendered visible rather than concealed.

In comparison to other senses, the sense of sight also appears to have one special quality. Eyesight and verbal development are clearly interconnected, and they develop in harmony with one another. According to Martin Jay (1993, 8), the universality of a visual experience can therefore never be assumed. He argues that a visual experience is positioned in culture through the means of language. The question of whether there are ways of seeing cross cultural borders is difficult and tends to be fragmented into a variety of sub-problems. We can, for instance, ask whether members of a community that is unfamiliar with photography can ever interpret photographs or whether the ability to interpret the medium of photography is the result of cultural learning. In the same vein, we can ask from a different standpoint: does a photograph, through its generic qualities, construct a visual order which the viewer must learn? It is hard to give an unambiguous answer to this, as I will discuss later in the chapter on visual literacy.

Time is an essential factor in looking. One assumption linked to looking is that when the lights are turned off, the projector is stopped or the advertisement has finished, looking also ceases. In fact this is seldom the case. The movie keeps spinning in the viewer's mind and can be tapped for discussion later. Hearing the score can instantly conjure up scenes as visual images, as happened to me when I bought the soundtrack of David Lynch's *The Straight Story* (1999). When I listen to Angelo Badalamenti's music, in my mind I can perceive the actors' expressions and movements as well as the landscapes where the events took place. Indeed, an important question is: *when does looking cease?* As what is seen earlier forms the foundation to what is seen now, new perceptions intertwine with the images left by the old ones—cognitive traces, if you will. It is also possible that one realizes having seen something only much later, after the fact, or the meaning of what was seen changes in one's mind. In other words: *looking is not a transient event but a constant and revisable process where earlier images, cultural experience and interaction are articulated.* Looking continues although the eyes are closed.

The durable concept that seeing is based on the eye's capacity to radiate light was born in antiquity. Most probably the belief was based on the perception that under certain conditions, the eye does indeed send rays of light by reflecting back light emanating from an external source. The eye's capacity to reflect light has also quite possibly contributed to the birth of mythologies connected to a look. The most well-known is the myth of the evil eye (*mal occhio*). I ran across the myth last when I was reading a story by the Finnish writer Mika Waltari to my daughter: *The Man with the Evil Eye* (1932).

The narrator of the story encounters a man with an evil eye at a streetcar stop. "It was as if a sudden, chilling gust of wind had sliced through the warm morning and I shivered of cold." The man was small, thin and grumpy-looking, but the force of his look was fatal: "He looked at the pigeons and they became agitated and their wings no longer glimmered and they took flight and fled, grey and ugly and pitiful, to backyards which, no doubt, were the right places for them anyway. (...) He glanced at windows which reflected the brilliant sunlight, and as his gaze moved from window to window the glimmer faded from them, they became entirely rigid and empty and poor. And the sun itself seemed to dim, as if concealed by a cloud even though there were no clouds in the sky, and the sky was no longer the joyful blue it was before but only dull and washed out blue."

The crux of Waltari's tale may lay in the notion that the evil eye is perhaps not a look directed to us from the outside, but a harsh look that we cast upon ourselves. If we surrender to the evil eye, we feel useless, incapacitated; we are left loveless. It is hard to avoid the notion that the narrator of the story describes soon after reflects the author's own emotions: "I remained there looking desolately at the words I had written, and a clear, calm, cool voice whispered in my ear: 'How can anybody write something so stupid—so bovine! Empty words, only empty words that try to strut all in a row and—alas!—contain no meaning at all.' I threw a startled glance around me but saw no-one. I was in the room all alone. But I imagined I clearly saw the Evil Eye. Wherever I looked, all went dark and cold before me, all that I had warmly loved." Here the evil eye is a human being's inner, punishing superego which does not allow its bearer a moment's peace to be content with his own doings or being, nor those of others. In Waltari's tale, the problematics of a look and a self-image culminate as hauntingly as in the texts of the theorists Georg Simmel, Jean-Paul Sartre or Jacques Lacan, all of whom will be introduced later.

In the context of this book, the moral of the evil eye stories is that the eye not only receives but also transmits. In this sense, eyesight differs from the other senses, which are solely receptive. However, I have often pondered whether being sensitized to human touch can be conveyed to another person through the sense of feeling. If this is the case, the sense of touch is also bi-directional, though perhaps not as clearly as the sense of sight. We can direct a hostile, loving, anxious, scrutinizing look to another person. Moreover, the eye is consciously better controlled than any other sensory organ. We can direct our look anywhere we want, select what we see and close the eyes from what we do not wish to see, although, at times, the unconscious gravitation of the eyes to their target and the unbearable urge to look can subvert conscious control. Sometimes we look without wanting to.

A LOOK IS A BOND

Let's imagine the following scene: the middle door of a bus opens. A man stands at the bus stop with a baby in a pram. He looks around to find help to lift the pram inside the bus. Exactly at that moment, most of the passengers spot something very interesting on the other side of the road and turn their looks away. Meeting the man's eyes would mean opening a channel of interaction which might force the person to react to the fact that help is needed. By turning one's eyes away it is possible to nullify the existence of the other person. Out of sight, out of mind!

Naturally, the passengers may have many reasons for their decision. Some may not tolerate a *man* asking for help to lift a pram. In Finnish culture a man only asks for help in cases of real distress, if even then. Some passengers may be too old to be of assistance. Some may have a hostile predisposition to pram people who block the aisles of buses. Some may experience it as difficult to offer a helping hand because doing so would render also them visible and exposed to other people's looks.

The situation is the sum of many essential features of how a look works. A look is linked to the recognition of another person as a participant in interaction. If I do not look at a person, I thus express an unwillingness to communicate with him or her. If I choose to receive the look of the man struggling with the pram, I make a promise to him with my own look. By exchanging looks we set our own roles in place and a momentary bond is constructed between us.

The German sociologist Georg Simmel (1858–1918) was interested in this kind of exchange of looks in the chapter "*Exkurs über die Soziologie der Sinne*" of his work *Soziologie* (1908). The sociology of the senses was important to Simmel because it is expressly through the senses that we position ourselves in relation to other people. The micro-sociological world construed through the senses is entwined in many ways, though undetected, with the macro-structure of the world. Sensory interaction between people is central to the functioning of the entire society. In this sense, eyesight is particularly precious to Simmel, and he indeed devotes a great deal of space to its analysis. (See Simmel 1968, 483–493; Simmel 1993)

According to Simmel (1968, 486), the eye has its own very special "sociological task," namely, the formation of a bond between individuals, in addition to the interaction based on reciprocal looks. The significance of the sense of sight has increased along with the birth of big cities. In city life, interaction is much more focused on seeing rather than hearing other people. This is not only due to the fact that on the streets of a small town one quite possibly runs into acquaintances with whom it is easy to stop for a chat. Simmel argues that one central reason for the dominance of the look in urban life is public transportation where people must look at each other silently for long periods of time.

Even though Simmel observes the expansion of the significance of eyesight in a broad framework—the stream of 19th century modernization—he focuses his analysis on the encounter of a dyad, as the interaction of two people. In this sense, it should be noted that Simmel's examination of a look does not extend to the area of the social "proper," which begins to form only when a third person enters the scene of interaction. However, the exchange of looks is the basis of interaction where people recognize and, at the same time, acknowledge one another as social actors. The bond of looks is temporary and ephemeral: the smallest deviation, the most furtive glance to the side, destroys the uniqueness of the bond. When looks meet, one cannot take without giving something in return: by looking, the viewer also exposes himself.

In addition to the other person's eyes, we also see his/her face, which has a very special meaning to Simmel.[1] He argues that the face provides us with a channel to another person's inner foundation (*inneren Fundamenten*) which is built on life experiences. The face is "the geometric place" for this knowledge; it is the symbol of all that a human being has collected throughout his personal history. We, however, do not always consciously recognize the story told by the face because our everyday activities are directed elsewhere and may therefore obscure the message. We can, for instance, be so engaged in a conversation that its contents usurp our conscious attention. Simmel also brings up the fact that the face can be ambiguous and even constrain interaction by leading to false interpretations.

Even though Simmel considers the system of reciprocal looks bound to eyesight to be central in terms of interaction, he certainly recognizes the significance of other senses. To him, the ear is an extremely selfish organ: it absorbs everything without giving anything back. Yet, it is through the ear that we receive the confirmation of what we see with our eyes. On the whole, Simmel emphasizes the teamwork of the senses and their ability to complement each other.

While a look constructs interaction between actors, a social bond, it also constructs the self of the participants of the interaction, their *subjectivity*. The significance of this kind of a bond can be easily conceptualized by thinking of how vital it is for a child to capture his/her parents' looks. When a child does something marvelous, s/he ceaselessly chants: "Look, daddy, look mommy!" By hijacking the parents' looks, the child reinforces his/her own identity.

When writing about a look, Simmel remains on strictly European terrain, where it is considered polite to look into the eyes of one's partner in conversation. An evasive look gives an odd, insecure or unreliable impression. There may be uncertainty about to whom the speaker is actually directing his/her words. To speak in one direction and look in another can suggest that the speaker is straying in his/her thoughts and is not concentrating on the subject. Directing one's look at the ground suggests submission, uncertainty or shyness.

The culturally conditioned nature of the reciprocal look becomes obvious when we leave Europe (see Argyle & Cook 1976, 29–34). The Navajo Indians learn early in childhood that it is inappropriate to look directly at one's partner in conversation. Amongst the South American Wituto and Bororo Indians, both the speaker and the listener let their eyes wander in the visual surroundings of the situation. In Niger, one is not allowed to look in the eyes of an older person or someone in a higher societal position. In the western visual orders it is polite to look in the eyes of people when we speak with them, but a prolonged look easily becomes a stare, which is a taboo. The taboo-like character of a look is linked to its presumed nature as a sexual message.

Simmel believed that the face opens up immediate access to another person's being. Michael and Deena Weinstein (1984) develop the idea in another direction: the face can just as well be a mask, which conceals and can be manipulated. The face can be molded. It can be covered or adorned with jewelry, make-up, facial hair, eye glasses or shades. The eyes of a person can also be covered against his/her own will. Covering the eyes of a prisoner sentenced to death embodies the relationship between the executioner and the doomed, which indeed is neither equal nor reciprocal.

THE BODY COMMUNICATES WITH THE EYE

Interaction built on the basis of the eyes forms one part of broader nonverbal communication. By looking, we detect body language and another person's physical appearance. The sphere of nonverbal communication also includes qualities of the voice (tone, strength, and pitch), touch and closeness. The forms of nonverbal communication often function reciprocally with a spoken language, thus forging a very multi-dimensional interactive situation. According to some studies, up to two-thirds of human interaction is based on nonverbal communication. Though there is reason to treat these kinds of generalizations with caution, it is apparent that interaction is strongly based on nonverbal messages. Laughing, smiling, grinning, crying all tell of the significance of the nonverbal. Yet, how come this area of communication is so very important?

Together with his fellow researchers, Judee K. Burgoon has discussed the topic in the book, *Nonverbal Communication: The Unspoken Dialogue* (1996). They argue (*ibid.*, 1) that nonverbal communication is significant because it is present everywhere: "Every communicative act carries with it nonverbal components. In face-to-face conversations, in public addresses, and in televised or videotaped presentations, all the nonverbal channels come into play." This is precisely what facial expressions, body posture, tone of voice, physical proximity, touch, physical appearance, and dress are. Even if a person tries not to express anything at all with his/her face, s/he expresses plenty. A poker face communicates resonantly and a resolve to stay silent is verbal communication at its best. I can see in my mind a news flash of the Middle East Peace Summit in 2000, hosted by president Bill Clinton, where the Israeli Prime Minister Ehud Barak and PLO leader Yasser Arafat shake hands. Clinton has to spread his arms and almost physically coerce the two parties of the negotiations to extend their hands to each other. The composition of the picture with its contrived smiles tells much more about the atmosphere of the meeting than the official press releases. Nonverbal messages can thus reveal the real state of affairs that is concealed behind verbal expression. However, nonverbal messages make misinterpretation possible just as well. A pleasant ambience and satisfaction reflected on the faces of the participants in an event may be staged in order to attain the desired impression. Any competent public relations agency is well aware of this and may exploit it in a briefing, for example, about a company's financial status. The worse the state of affairs, the more important it is to communicate optimism through body language.

Secondly, Burgoon et al. argues (*ibid.*, 5) that "nonverbal behaviors may form a universal language system." In the sphere of contemporary cultural studies, this kind of universalism sounds rather dubious: is it not the aim to try to understand phenomena expressly in their cultural context? Burgoon nevertheless claims (*ibid.*) that certain nonverbal signals like smiling, crying, pointing, caressing and staring are in use all over the world. "They allow people to communicate with one another at the most basic level regardless of their familiarity with the prevailing language system. Such nonverbal actions thus transcend cultural differences, forming a kind of universal language." The argument is on the daring side, even if language in this connection is understood metaphorically, that is, in the same sense as in the expression "the language of love."

Even if all the above-mentioned forms of nonverbal communication were universally valid, they might still take on different meanings in the diverse cultural settings and situations in which they are interpreted. Laughter, for example, is considered a strong signal of joy but it can also express extreme sorrow, fear or rejection. In any event, we can safely conclude that people can communicate using the language of gestures even if they do not understand one another's verbal language. Smiling to another person on a first encounter gives quite a universal signal in its meanings, even though exceptions may exist. It can be thus argued that nonverbal communication is more universal than communication based on written or oral language. This is self-evident to anyone who has tried to explain something to another person without a common language. However, even if one shares a common language, it is sometimes necessary to draw a picture to make oneself understood. Ultimately, Burgoon et al. underline the cultural nature of nonverbal communication.

The culture-bound nature of gesture language was manifested concretely when the then vice-president Richard Nixon undertook a goodwill tour to Latin America in 1958 (see *ibid.*, 24). As he was descending from the airplane, Nixon made an A-OK-gesture with his both hands, that is, he formed the circle O with his thumb and the index finger while the other fingers fanned out from the palm. The photographs of the gesture were spread in the news media. Unfortunately for Nixon, the OK gesture has pretty much the same meaning in some Latin American countries as flipping the middle finger has for North Americans.

Nonverbal communication precedes speech in the development of both the species and the individual. Many animals can nonverbally communicate with one another. This is valid also in the development of the human species, which means that "we are inherently programmed to attend first and foremost to nonverbal signals" (*ibid.*, 6). Before learning to speak, a child communicates with a multiplicity of nonverbal means with other people, particularly with his or her primary caretaker. According to Burgoon and his collaborators, nonverbal signals are particularly clear when a human being resorts to primal behaviors, such as in situations of stress and fear. Though this kind of thinking is fraught by the danger to biologize human behaviors—that is, to reduce cultural behavioral models to biology—there is also something that rings very true about it. A gush of primitive anger floods the blood with adrenalin, breaks through cultural behavioral norms, fixes one's glare at the opponent, changes the stature of the body and makes the face flush.

A child learns to communicate with others first and foremost through touching, closeness, swaying, looking—in general, through the medium of the body. The lingual system develops much later. This kind of communication is vitally important to the development of the child's sense of body and language. We never abandon these early forms of nonverbal communication, but they become more complex, cultivated and extended, as well as incorporated into verbal communication, as we grow up. The British author and researcher on images, John Berger (1977, 7), describes the meaning of seeing in human development in the foreword of his much-quoted work *Ways of Seeing*:

> Seeing comes before words. The child looks and recognizes before it can speak. But there is also other sense in which seeing becomes before words. It is seeing which establishes our place in the surrounding world; we explain that world with words, but words can never undo the fact that we are surrounded by it. The relation between what we see and what we know is never settled. Each evening we see the sun set. We know that the earth is turning away. Yet the knowledge, the explanation, never quite fits the sights.

One of the most important qualities of nonverbal communication is our ability to express things which are beyond reach of our verbal expression or which we do not want to say aloud. Hugging or smiling to someone can convey meanings which might actually be trivialized if said aloud. Through looks, it is possible to assess another person—open channels, as was illustrated in the earlier example of the man with the pram—but, at the same time, they are susceptible to misinterpretation. A surprised, confused, even unwelcoming look can be interpreted as a sign of interest. Though nonverbal messages can be treacherous, people usually trust them more than verbal expressions, particularly if they give a different message than the spoken words.

Touch, tone of voice and closeness are important forms of nonverbal communication, but the most essential one is body language, which in sensory terms belongs to the realm of the eye. Eyesight is without doubt the most central sense of nonverbal communication. The term *body language* naturally evokes the notion of a system similar to spoken or written language. Here, there is no reason to speculate about the ways that body language does or does not resemble verbal language, but suffice it to say that even though body language shares certain common features with verbal language, it lacks many of its essential qualities. For example, body language is often iconic in semiotic terms; that is, the form of the expression resembles its content. When I tell a fishing tale, my arms stretch the further the bigger the lie is. Expressions of verbal language are iconic only in the exceptions. I will return to semiotics in the fourth chapter, where I discuss the semiotic qualities of the "language" of the photograph and traditional writing.

In any case, body language is abundant. The face is only one site, but when considering the totality of human interaction, it can be seen as the most central part of body language as a whole. Different quantitative estimates have been conducted on this question: physiological examinations have shown that facial muscles alone can produce 20,000 different expressions (Burgoon et al. 1996, 33).

The signals of the facial area can be roughly divided into three groups: static, slow and rapid signals (*ibid.*, 284). Static signals include the bone structure and the complexion, though also they can be altered by means of surgery or make-up. Slow signals change but this happens over a relatively long time period. Furrows and other signs of ageing, Simmelian markers of life experience, develop on the skin. Because youth is so highly esteemed in the western societies, many people battle against their own biology and strive to make themselves over to be a part of the visual order of youth, a wrinkle-free existence. The psychological connection is deep: joining the visual order of youth makes the soul grow younger as well.

Static and slow facial signals are important in facial area communication, but in a culture that is enraptured with change, rapid signals are naturally the most interesting. They are also very revealing. They cannot be hidden under make-up like wrinkled skin, even though they can be played with as well. I remember from childhood, as well as from a few situations in the adult world, how disappointment forced the corners of my mouth downwards and tears welled. At the same time, I was naturally ashamed and feared that my disappointment would show. So, as my face fell, I directed my eyes to the ground and flushed. These signals were certainly available for interpretation by anyone nearby. Strong emotions, such as fear, disgust, hatred, love and happiness are visible from afar, whereas more subtle feelings like envy may require skilful interpretation. Moreover, there are many everyday expressions that we notice but remain unaware of their effect on us. One of these is a smile: is it benevolent, mischievous, condescending, amused, tender, sarcastic or perhaps even playful?

The expressive register of the face alone is thus overwhelming. Other physical features can also communicate resonantly in the nonverbal register, which is obvious when we think how much people work on their outer appearance. People always send messages with their looks, whether they intend to or not, and normative beauty ideals can often have a cruel impact, for example, on the identity of young people. It is not merely a question of harmless play if a child is bullied in school because s/he does not fit into trousers two sizes smaller and thus assimilate into the prevailing norms that dictate how s/he should look. Hence, body language—similar to other forms of nonverbal communication—is structured; it contains visual orders which have an impact on the actions, behavior and formation of individual identities. People maintain the visual orders of body language by molding their body with exercise, make-up and the way they dress.

It is for this reason that understanding nonverbal communication and its cultural meanings is a decisive part of visual literacy. It may be that this is an area of visual literacy that can be learned only in a restrictive sense by reading books and contemplating images. Rather, it is developed as a sensitivity that emerges from experience, as an outcome of observing people and pondering meanings of different visual representations.

Simmelian interaction and nonverbal communication, as far as they remain in sensory terms on the terrain of the eye, focus our attention on the eye. They are based on concrete and often reciprocal looking. However, looking also has other dimensions, as the tale by Mika Waltari showed us. The story's evil eye is certainly the concrete look of the man standing in the bus stop, but it is also an anonymous Gaze which is targeted at a human being from outside him or herself. French philosopher Jean-Paul Sartre (1905–1980) and psychoanalyst Jacques Lacan (1901–1981) were particularly interested in this gaze and its effects on us.

PEEPING CAUSES SHAME

I am peeping through a keyhole. I am absorbed in and completely enthralled by what I see. Suddenly, I hear voices behind me and become painfully conscious of myself peeping. I blush, straighten myself out and pull myself away from the vista.

The episode is a modification of an event that Jean-Paul Sartre describes to the reader in his book, *Being and Nothingness* (1943). In his work, Sartre also addresses the problematics of the Gaze. The entire analysis of the Gaze serves Sartre's philosophical passion and is subordinate to the philosophical system he created. Unfortunately, it is not possible to delve deeper into that issue here. I focus selectively on the part that addresses the Gaze and leave Sartre's complex philosophical problems for another time (Theunissen 1984, 217–218; see also Catalano 1985, 149–168). Contrary to Simmel, the social bond that a look establishes between two people has very little significance to Sartre. He indeed makes a radical move and detaches the look from the optic organ, the eye. Sartre (1992, 346) writes: "Of course, what *most often* manifests a look is the convergence of two ocular globes in my direction. But the look will be given just as well on occasion when there is rustling of branches, or the sound of a footstep followed by silence, or the slight opening of a shutter, or a light movement of a curtain."

I can therefore interpret the slight movement of the curtain in the neighboring house as a sign of me being the object of someone's look. Of course, I cannot be absolutely sure whether I am being looked at or not. The sense of being looked at does not require a definite certainty that some specific physical human being sees me. However, 'a look' directed towards me gives me cause to pay heed to my behavior. Even though this kind of a Gaze may not have its source in someone's eyes, it does have an owner that Sartre describes with the term "the Other". Sartre characterizes the Other in many ways, often quite metaphorically and ambiguously. It is distinguished by immediate presence, it is not from this world, and "in the first place, he is the being toward whom I do not turn my attention. He is the one who looks at me and at whom I am yet not looking, the one that delivers me to myself unraveled but without revealing himself, the one who is present to me as directing at me but never as the object of my direction." (Sartre 1992, 360) According to Sartre, one feature of our consciousness is being for others (*être-pour-autrui*). The Other is a fundamental condition for me to be able to become conscious of myself in totality. The keyhole episode is one example of this. As I am absorbed in the vision before me, I am not conscious of my own existence. But when I hear footsteps behind me, I become embarrassingly conscious of myself, or, to be more precise, of myself peeping. The presence of the Other awakens my self-consciousness.

Even though being for others is necessary, it is also tragic because it makes my existence dependent on being an object. The Gaze of the Other enslaves me and restricts my being, as well as evokes feelings of shame. Sartre writes (*ibid.*, 350) how shame is "(…) shame of *self*; it is the recognition of the fact that I *am* indeed that object which the Other is looking at and judging. I can be ashamed only as my freedom escapes me in order to become a given object." Sartre uses nudity as an example: when naked, we are extremely defenseless. When we get dressed, we can simultaneously conceal our state as an object. When I become the object of the Gaze of the Other, I also lose part of my own freedom, my possibilities. The sense of shame emerges from being conscious of this state. When I become aware of the Other's Gaze, I become conscious of the freedom of the Other that is greater than my own freedom. In addition to growing into an object of the Gaze of the Other, I can possibly become an instrument that the Other can exploit. Hence, I always carry the awareness with me that I can become seen. When I cover my naked body with clothes before answering the doorbell, I do not usually think of any certain person who could see me. I wear clothes because some internal, yet simultaneously external force makes me conceal my body from the looks of others. In fact, the expression *outer look* precisely demonstrates what the question really is: my body is the object of a certain look which is outside me but which has an impact on my consciousness and activities.

Sartre's understanding of a look fundamentally differs from Simmel's views. Simmel understands a reciprocal look as a phenomenon that forms an imperative basis for social interaction. For Sartre, the problem of a look and looking is linked with human existence and the preconditions that the Other sets for it. Where

Simmel's look builds a bridge between two people, Sartrean Gaze builds a bridge to its individual object's self-awareness. While the Gaze of the Other renders us conscious of ourselves, it also objectifies, limits and alienates. The most profound difference from the Simmelian look emerges when Sartre detaches the look from concrete looking and makes it a force that is impersonal and, paradoxically, separate from the eye. The focal point is thus removed from the subject as a viewer to the general *visibility* of the subject.

It is not hard to find practical applications of the Gaze of the Other. The *panopticon* springs immediately to mind. It is a concept originally invented by Jeremy Bentham and analyzed by Michel Foucault in his famous book, *Discipline and Punish*.

The panopticon is a prison where the cells are positioned in such a way that it is possible to see into all of them from the control room located in the central tower, but it is not possible to see into the tower from any of the cells. This kind of controlling look that objectifies its target is simultaneously abstract and concrete. The following quote from Foucault (1977, 201–202) illustrates the interrelation of visibility, power and control:

> Bentham laid down the principle that power should be visible and unverifiable. Visible: the inmate will constantly have before his eyes the tall outline of the central tower from which he is spied upon. Unverifiable: the inmate must never know whether he is looked at at any moment; but he must be sure that he may always be so. (...) The Panopticon is a machine for dissociating the see/being seen dyad: in the peripheric ring, one is totally seen, without ever seeing; in the central tower, one sees everything without ever being seen.

Through the means of current technology, it is possible to transform any prison into a panopticon. Structural solutions are unnecessary; a surveillance camera in each cell suffices. The use of camera surveillance in banks, cashpoints, streets, public spaces and so forth make the entire society into a panopticon where individuals are reduced to objects of monitoring. If such a system includes video recording, the individual's location in the controlled area can also be verified after the fact. The question then is no longer whether I obey the preconditions of the Gaze right now, but whether I am doing something right now that may in the future be turned to my disadvantage. Surveillance based on the Gaze can be effective also when simulated. The inhabitants of a semi-detached house in my neighborhood installed a broken video camera in their backyard accompanied by a sign "Video Surveillance."

Deena and Michael Weinstein (1984, 359–360) remind us of another everyday phenomenon which—contrary to the Gaze of the Other—is looking at its most concrete: staring. According to the Weinsteins, staring is an example of a *conscious* wish to render someone an object. They use children's staring contests as examples. The winner of a staring contest is the one who, through his/her own stare, forces the opponent to divert his/hers. They could have just as well looked for an example in the adult world. It is not very unusual that people take the measure of each other by looking. In this case, the one who gives up first and allows his/her look to fall surrenders and acknowledges the other's superiority. Staring can also be unconscious and hence paradoxical. Who has not caught himself staring at a disabled person? Some stare unashamedly, judging the person to be 'disabled' by their stare, but most of us probably realize to our own shame that we are staring, a viewpoint that Sartre ignores. When I objectify, for instance, a disabled person as the target of my look I, at the same time, expose myself to the Gaze of the Other who can catch me out for this shameful deed. If the object of my look is able to hijack it and throw it straight back at me, the catastrophe is complete. I am now the object of both the stare of him/her and the Gaze of the Other and shrink under my twofold shame.

THE GAZE AND THE SARDINE CAN

There is a story connected to the look that was written just a couple of decades after Sartre's principal work was published. The protagonist, psychoanalyst Jacques Lacan, decided to familiarize himself with "real life" and visited a fishing boat on the west coast of France. "At that time, Brittany was not as industrialized as it is now. There were no trawlers. The Fisherman went out in his own frail craft at his own risk. It was this risk, this danger, that I loved to share," is how Lacan (1977b, 95) described his motives. In the deep sea, the fisherman, Petit-Jean, pointed at a floating, glimmering sardine can object and taunted Lacan: "You can see that? Do you see it? Well, it doesn't see you!" (*Ibid*). There was perhaps no deeper meaning intended in the gibe, but as an intellectual, Lacan promptly started to search for meaning where there was none. The episode continued to ferment in Lacan's mind and ended up in his 1964 lectures.

Immense meanings began to be construed around the glimmering sardine can in Lacan's texts where he contemplates on looking and the Gaze.[2] Of course, the can does not see Lacan. However, the words of Petit-Jean assume a certain concrete meaning if we think that the can 'looks' at Lacan by directing rays of light into his eyes. Similar to Sartre, Lacan thus robs the human actor of the gaze and ironically hands it over to the sardine can. Before a closer examination of the sardine can, I would like to make some general remarks on Lacan.

Lacan does not think that subjectivity is formed solely through the visual. If anybody, Lacan was the one who recognized human beings as verbal actors. However, the visual has its place in Lacan's thinking on subjectivity. Researchers on the cinema have utilized the idea of the mirror stage, which Lacan developed in the 1930s. In the mirror stage a child identifies with the closest being through the eye and does not recognize him/herself in it. The notion of the mirror stage has raised a great deal of debate both in cinematic research and elsewhere (see e.g. Tudor 1999), but a more detailed discussion of the notion is not possible here. It is rather ironic that the mirror stage has stood on such a firm ground in the analysis of the viewer's experience of a movie, even though Lacan's actual contemplations of the gaze lay elsewhere. Pia Sivenius (1997) draws attention to one thing that is useful to keep in mind. Lacan does not have an actual *theory* of the Gaze; the same is true also for Simmel and Sartre. Lacan explores the surroundings of the Gaze; he utilizes and develops the thinking of Sigmund Freud, Maurice Merleau-Ponty and Sartre—often depressingly verbosely.[3]

German literary theorist Samuel Weber (1991) has discussed Lacan's opacity. Weber writes: "What his texts give voice to and in a certain sense 'stage' is not simply something represented, an object that would be self-identical, but is itself representation, translation, staging" (Weber 1991, 1). With his way of writing, Lacan thus focuses the reader's attention on the fact that all meanings given to presentations are agreements, which are historical, and, therefore, changeable. In this case, Lacan needs neologisms (e.g. *objet a*), which indicate the vacant points in the textual context they inhabit—the void of meanings. This aspiration, as I conceive it, is connected to Lacan's views of the possibilities of textual critique. Hence all interpretations of Lacan are similarly limited to how still images are restricted in relation to a movie; moreover, to precisely such a movie that has no actual plots with closure. Lacan's strategy has also led to unfortunate results: a psychoanalyst has become a maze of meanings, *Lacan*, which chases many readers away.

It is possible to at least attempt to understand the Look of the sardine can that glimmers in Lacan's thoughts through the following diagrams (Fig 3.1) that represent the relationships between the Gaze, the subject and the screen (Lacan 1977b, 91; see also Silverman 1996, 132).

The tip of the first triangle is the geometric point (*point géométral*), from which the perception takes place. The object (*objet*) of seeing is reached through an image. This is unproblematic *per se*, perhaps even familiar. The viewer is located at a point where he observes the space in perspective. The world opens up according to the laws of geometry and becomes crystallized in the image.

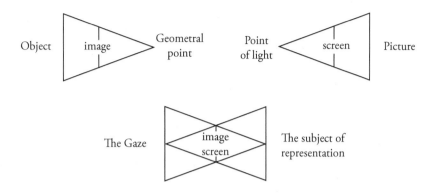

Figure 3.1 *Relations between the Gaze, subject and the screen (écran).*

John Berger (1977,16) has characterized the cone of the Gaze most felicitously: "It is like a beam from a lighthouse—only instead of light traveling outwards, appearances travel in. The conventions called those appearances *reality*. Perspective makes the single eye the centre of the visible world. Everything converges on to the eye as to the vanishing point of infinity. The visible world is arranged for the viewer as the universe was once thought to be arranged for God. According to the convention of the perspective there is no visual reciprocity."

Berger writes from the Renaissance doctrine of perspective. The "image" of the first diagram could indeed be replaced by the framework created by the art theorist Leon Battista Alberti (1404–1472) of the Renaissance era, through the means of which the artist could outline a representation of the world in accurate perspective. The "image" could just as well be replaced by Albrecht Dürer's metal grid through which the artist looks (see p. 25). The grid formed a kind of an assisting net of lines which helped the artist to draw a picture in a correct perspective.

In Lacan's mind, however, this kind of thinking was defective. When the eye is situated in the geometric point, it separates itself from something that Lacan calls *the function of seeingness*. The notion is reflected by the thought that I see only from one point but I am seen from everywhere. Like Sartre, Lacan thus detaches the gaze from the eye and in doing so, knocks the individual viewer off his throne. The viewer becomes the object of seeing. This is illustrated by Lacan's second triangle. Its tip forms "point of light" (*point lumineux*), its base "picture" (*tableau*) and between them is the level called screen (*écran*).[4] Again, the picture is a metaphor for the human being who is the object of the gaze: when I am looked at, I form "a picture" or am a part of it. In the third diagram, the first and the second triangles are placed one upon the other. "Picture" has become "the subject of representation," "screen" and "image" have become one and the gaze has replaced the point of light. Along with other things, the diagram is intended to emphasize how looking and being looked at take place simultaneously.

Lacan defines the gaze as follows:

> In the scopic field, the gaze is outside, I am looked at, that is to say, I am a picture. This is the function that is found at the heart of the institution of the subject in the visible. What determines me, at the most profound level, in the visible is the gaze that is outside. It is through the gaze that I enter light and it is from the gaze that I receive its effects. Hence it comes about that gaze is the instrument through which light is embodied and through which—if you will allow me to use a word, as I often do, in a fragmented form—I am *photo-graphed*. (Lacan 1977b, 106)

> In our relation to things, in so far as this relation is constituted by the way of vision, and ordered in the figures of representation, something slips, passes, is transmitted, from stage to stage, and is always to some degree eluded in it—that is what we call the gaze. (*Ibid.*, 73)

It is somewhat possible to grip the meaning of the gaze and the screen when it is examined through two concepts: mimicry (mimesis) and Freudian screen memory (*Deckerinnerung*).

In connection with his analysis of the gaze, Lacan relies on Roger Caillois as he discusses the capacity of some species to assimilate with their environment; that is, their mimetic reactions. Animals and organisms may take cover from their predators by changing to resemble their surroundings. According to Caillois's views, it is not a question of a defensive reaction or adaptation, but rather the degeneration of a species. The creatures merge into an inseparable part of their surroundings as if relinquishing their own existence. Lacan subscribes at least partly to Caillois's interpretations of mimesis. Biologists may have their own say of Caillois's views, but biological accuracy is not relevant here. What is essential is that the capacity of a species to transform to resemble its surroundings is a kind of photography; the surrounding world is depicted on the skin of the creature like shapes are depicted on film. When we look at this in terms of light, light in fact photo-graphs the imprint of the surroundings on the skin of the creature. Moreover, because for Lacan light and the gaze walk hand in hand, it is expressly the gaze that photo-graphs the creature and simultaneously places it as a part of the picture, its surroundings.

How did Lacan (*ibid.*, 106) put it? "What determines me, at the most profound level, in the visible, is the gaze that is outside. It is through the gaze that I enter light and it is from the gaze that I receive its effects. Hence it comes about that the gaze is the instrument through which light is embodied and through which— if you will allow me to use a word, as I often do, in a fragmented form—I am *photo-graphed*." This is where the screen enters. In terms of the earlier example it could be said, though perhaps a little crudely, that the screen is the visual shape of the surroundings that is depicted on the skin of the creature. The screen positions and merges the creatures into the picture by forming just the right kind of texture, a pattern, on their skin. If this notion is transferred onto culture, we can think like this: We are all in subordination to the Gaze directed at us which determines our own visibility. However, our visibility cannot be arbitrary; it is structured, bound by rules and dictated by visual orders. For instance, in a funeral we are allowed to be seen only in strictly regulated attire. Hence, the screen is the array of all the possible visual forms that we can assume in a funeral, the visual order of a certain situation. A dark suit is fine; a t-shirt does not fit into the picture. "And if I am something in a picture, I am in the form of the screen," Lacan (*ibid.*) remarked.

Like mimetic creatures, we can only surrender to the position allotted to us by the screen of the Gaze. The conception is merciless. We have no possibility but to become like our environment, to assimilate into the visual order, or we are in trouble. Lacan himself sensed this pressure when he figured out the social dimension of the gibe about the sardine can. The men in the fishing boat were looking at him but did not in fact consent to see him. This is demonstrated in Petit-Jean's gibe. "The point of this little story, as it had occurred to my partner, the fact that he found it so funny and I less so, derives from the fact that, if I am told a story like that one, it is because I, at that moment—as I appeared to those fellows who were earning their livings with great difficulty, in the struggle what for them was pitiless nature—looked like nothing on earth. In short, I was rather out of place in the picture," Lacan (*ibid.*, 95–96) sums up.

However, he impresses upon us the fact that a human being can distinguish between his existence and the picture of that existence, its visual being. This opens up the possibility to choose not to be part of visual orders. The screen is then not only a one-way force that shackles the visibility of a human being, but it grows into a point of mediation through which it is possible to appear to the Gaze in a certain way. I can become just the picture preordained by the visual order (*écran*), but internally I can be something else. I can dress deliberately in a provocative manner. I can exaggerate just for kicks. I can even make the screen visible by keeping up small talk about my attire in a situation where people firmly believe it is just the same as what they look like. Fraud, masquerading, breaking the picture, play, adaptation and negotiation are ways of action made possible by *écran*.

However, the screen does not only regulate the ways of how a person is seen. It also provides the bulk of such images with which a person wants to identify. The Gaze "invites" people to identify through the screen with different pictures. What we look at and how we ourselves are objects of looking are therefore intrinsically intertwined. If I want to be *rock*, I identify with the black leather coat imagery and buy myself a leather coat. The screen embodies the visual code system through which we both identify with guises and ourselves look a certain way to the outer world. Thus the screen works also as a means of distinguishing: we categorize others as belonging to certain groups, for example, by their visual being. Kaja Silverman (1996, 135) sums up the dynamic of the screen and the Gaze in the following way: "The screen represents the site at which gaze is defined for particular society, and is consequently responsible both for the way in which the inhabitants of that society experience the gaze's effects, and for much of the seeming particularity of that society's visual regime."

In Lacan's thinking, however, the screen is not as "culturally" oriented as could be concluded from the reading above. Over a hundred years ago, Sigmund Freud (1856–1939) wrote a rather brief text "Screen memories" (1899), which has an obvious connection with Lacan's concept of the screen.[5] Screen memories overpower real memories. Screen memories have the ingredients of the original memories, but a screen memory is always remolded by fantasy, repression and displacement. Freud reminisces about his own childhood and disguises a certain incident as a memory of an imaginary patient. He then has a discussion with the patient—himself—how the memory, indifferent in itself—transpires as a symbolic entity that reflects the central elements of life: sustenance and love.

Freud considers screen memory only in relation to childhood experiences and their impact on what is remembered. However, he discloses that adult experiences can also transform a memory into a screen memory. Furthermore: "It may indeed be questioned whether we have any memories at all *from* our childhood: memories *relating to* our childhood may be all that we possess" (Freud 1992, 322). Hence, all our memories are simultaneously both a gauze and screen on which the past is reflected insofar as it is molded by the present. What is important here is the simultaneous nature of screen memory both as a gauze that shrouds and obscures the original memory, and as its projection surface, a screen, although of a rather special kind. Are there not two kinds of screens: one that aims at reflecting back all light directed to it as completely as possible. In this case, the projector is on the same side of the screen as the viewer. The other kind of screen is located between the projector and the viewer. It becomes a semi-transparent weave with the intention to give the light the possibility to form an image, as well as simultaneously prevent the excessive flooding of light to the eye, causing it to become blinded. It dims the projector's gaze directed to us so that seeing and forming an image would become possible. Screen memory similarly both dims the uncontrolled glare of the unconscious and structures the conscious image that is more or less clear in our mind. The connection between the *écran* and screen memory brings with it the entire dynamics of the unconscious with its slips, repressions and condensations to Lacan's conception of the gaze.

Kaja Silverman's interpretation of the *écran* as a means through which people experience the impact of the Gaze within a certain visual field brings the *écran* quite close to the concept of visual order in this book. Visual order determines how we appear to other people, what kinds of things are rendered visible in the first place, what we do in fact see—whether the objects of our scrutiny are pictures or, say, other people. Like the *écran*, visual orders are not so dominant that they could not be subjected to change, interrupted or unscrupulously exploited.

IN THE FIELD OF THE GAZE

In her article on the Gaze, Pia Sivenius (1997, 53) remarks that there is something in the world that is always awaiting a seeing person, just as language awaits a speaking person. But what is it out there that awaits the seeing person?

The world of reciprocal looks is certainly out there awaiting us. It forms an essential part of human interaction, nonverbal communication and visual orders. The world of optics that monitors our minds and bodies is also out there. This optics is constructed as part of the anonymous Gaze and the visual orders that are formed through it. We are also awaited by many artefacts and presentations that feed the eye, on which we focus our look either consciously—or, as happens most often—dictated by our unconscious desires and predilections. A human being can identify him/herself with only certain images and mental impressions while others are rejected, often not even seen. We only see what we can see while we can only talk about what we are able to talk about.

The essential question indeed is *why we see what we see*. All this visibility and invisibility is not arbitrary motion. The visual has its orders and structures which can be condensed into the culturalized *écran*. It dictates the preconditions for our visibility, visual identifications and, at the same time, enables play with visual imagery, resistance, if you will.

When Simmel's, Sartre's and Lacan's thinking is condensed into the bare essentials, three fields emerge that concern the formation of the visual field. They all have an impact on every looking situation and partially overlap.

The first field is constructed on the basis of the reciprocal look. There people encounter one another through looks and the look grows into one element of interaction. As became evident earlier, this kind of look has a powerful impact on a child's socialization process as well as on the interaction in general. The reciprocal look is culturally determined and has its own norms, which must be paid heed to in a similar way to the other preconditions that influence activity. This look could be depicted by the diagram A, in which a bond is construed between two subjects (see Fig. 3.2).

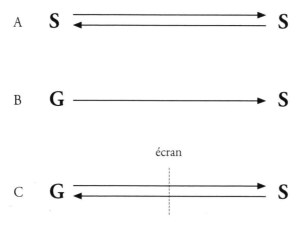

Figure 3.2 *The dynamics of looking and being looked at.*

Understanding a look as *a bond and an interaction* is fruitful but limited, because it ties the look to a subject. Sartre radicalizes the look by detaching it from the eye and transferring it to outside of the viewer. Hence, the central place is occupied not by the viewer's own look but in *the Gaze of the Other* (Fig. 3.2, B). However, both Simmel's and Sartre's conception of the look is bipolar. The question is that of the interaction between two subjects, or the Other and a human being. Lacan brings a third, mediating actor to the scene, the *écran* or *screen* (Fig. 3.2, C).

Along with the last diagram visual literacy cannot be understood only as a relationship between the viewer of the picture (subject) and the target of looking (picture, object). Every individual participates in different visual orders both in the 'pictorial' and 'non-pictorial' reality, in which s/he is both a subject and an object of looking. When looking at pictures, a person always looks at them as part of some broader visual order, which in turn at least partially determines what the person ultimately sees in the pictures. People can also use pictures to build up their own visibility, to give a certain impression of themselves to other people or to that anonymous Gaze that strives to position everyone as part of a certain visual order.

On this basis, we can see that visual literacy is the capacity to understand and analyze one's own position as a part of different visual orders. An interpretation of a pictorial representation—be it a photograph, movie or the screen of the computer—is only one part of this broader visual literacy.

PUBLIC ENEMY: ONCE AGAIN

I acquired the Public Enemy poster mentioned in the previous chapter when I was in my mid-thirties. How come the poster ended up on my kitchen wall? What do I communicate through the poster and its visual orders?

The first visual order is connected to the form of representation. Almost everyone who looks at it recognizes—consciously or unconsciously—that it is a poster. To be more exact, it is a band poster, which links associations to the band through visual meanings that are very carefully conceived. The poster is based on a photograph, which is in black-and-white, heavily contrasted and lean in its tones. This connects the poster to the genre of the documentary photograph and its visual meanings. Though the people that appear in the picture have been positioned very carefully, the picture gives the impression of a militant rap posse yanked straight off the street. The genre of documentary photography embraces the notions of life-likeness and realism: its intention is to depict reality accurately and without distortion.[6] In fact, black-and-white quality enhances the credibility of a documentary photograph. This is slightly paradoxical. Shouldn't a credible photograph be in color instead because the world itself is full of color? Black-and-white as a marker of realism is partially due to the truth functions that are linked to photography in general and partially to the specific history of photography. The concept of documentarism was not introduced into the history of photography before the 1930s, when, for example, photographers employed by New Deal work programs, such as the Farm Security Administration (FSA), began to be characterized as documentarists (see e.g. Tagg 1988; Solomon-Godeau 1991).

The goal of the FSA program was to record the living conditions in the rural areas of the USA. They used black-and-white film, and also later black-and-white has been linked to the visual order of documentarist photography. By working in black-and-white, many documentarist photographers have distinguished themselves from lay camera owners who take their Sunday snaps in color. In fact, colors found their way onto the terrain of documentarist photography as late as the 1980s.

This visual order of documentarism lends special credibility to the poster and simultaneously connects it to the meanings of the color black in the rock dress code, and, of course, to rap as the rebellion of African-American men. Through realism effects, a black-and-white document of African-American rappers reinforces their street credibility, which is also an essential part of rock mythology.

The black-and-white quality of the picture is articulated with how African-American men are usually depicted in public imagery. According to cultural studies researcher Stuart Hall, representations of African-American men, the construction of the visual order of the Black man, have signified their separation from white men. The construction of this difference has drawn from different stereotypes—clichés and one-sided generalizations—about African-American men and Blacks in general. In his article, "The Spectacle of the 'Other' ", Hall raises many ways of stereotyping Blacks. According to Hall (1997, 251) , the Hollywood movie industry provides plenty of material to contemplate the multiple ways of representing African-American men because it was "the popular art form of the first half of the twentieth century." Hall argues that the American film continues to maintain ways of representation of the Blacks that originate from slavery even now, though somewhat diluted. As Hall counts off the different stereotypes, he relies on Donald Bogle's book, *Toms, Coons, Mulattoes, Mammies and Bucks: An Interpretive History of Blacks in American Films*, where five different stereotypes are distinguished (Bogle 1996, 3–18).

The first stereotype is The Tom, which origin can be traced back to Edwin S. Porter's film *Uncle Tom's Cabin* (1903). "Always as toms are chased, harassed, hounded, flogged, enslaved, and insulted, they keep faith, n'er turn against their white massas, and remain hearty, submissive, stoic, generous, selfless, and oh-so-very kind", Bogle (*ibid.*, 6–7) writes. Toms dominated the American film imagery but they had serious competition from the another figure called the Coon. A typical coon is a pickaninny, harmless, "little screwball creation whose eyes popped, whose hair stood on the end with the least excitement, and whose antics were pleasant and diverting" (*ibid.*). The third type is the Tragic Mulatto, mixed-race woman, beautiful and sexually attractive and also suitable, thanks for her partly white blood, to white men, too. The Mammy is the fourth stereotype, a female figure who usually is big, fat and cantankerous—often a house-servant. The last type is the Black Buck. They are "big, baadddd niggers, oversexed and savage, violent and frenzied as their lust of white flesh." (*Ibid.*, 13)

There are many traces of the last-mentioned type in the imagery of today's young African-Americans, which is manifested expressly in *gangsta rap* and "niggas with attitude" bands. Black youth themselves have adopted the imagery of the "bad nigga" as they construct their identity and their own ways of separating themselves from "good Blacks," white culture and rock. At the same time, the "bad nigga" imagery functions as a stereotype of African-American men and connects it to the original historical caricature.

The meanings of the poster are incorporated into that stereotype. An African-American man is aggressive, brassy, and cannot adjust to rules created by others. Many of the picture's details communicate precisely this. First, there is the direct pose which accentuates consciousness of the camera and, at the same time, of the viewer of the picture. The African-American men do not simply acquiesce to the documenting camera. They use representation as an instrument to create their own visual order. Or, strictly speaking, the direct pose gives an impression of this. As I mentioned earlier, it is also possible that the entire picture is very carefully constructed to aim precisely at this kind of an impression—regardless of what the members of Public Enemy actually want to communicate. In addition to the frontal pose, the wearing of black shades is not only a rock cliché (Blues Brothers imagery and associations connected to it), but also an effective way of concealing a look and hence, rather paradoxically, emphasizing it. Shades protect one from being blinded and from the looks of others. The men station themselves brazenly before the viewer, block the way, but scorn the reciprocal look and thus communication. Black, audacious and uncommunicative! The third gesture that supports the imagery of the "bad nigga" emerges from the background of the picture, where one of the band members has raised his leather-clad fist into a Black Panther salute, which ultimately links the meanings of the picture to an inseparable part of the war against racism and discrimination. The fourth element supporting the imagery is naturally the uniform-like clothing, which, however, may also bear (self) ironic meanings. It indicates military order and organization. This is further supported by the band's logo located on the top of the poster, which depicts a human being as a shooting target. The spatial grouping of the band members can also be counted in the imagery of the "bad nigga." They block a narrow alleyway: who must give way?

There are only men in the picture. This reinforces the impression that rap is music made specifically by men. The picture is a kind of a constellation of mythical hyper-masculinity, which is capable, heterosexual and Black. Is it then so that African-American men have introduced certain central racializing elements as part of their struggle—established and cliché-like conceptions? Historically speaking, if the explanation by Kobena Mercer and Isaac Julien is correct, this interpretation would not be too far-fetched. According to them, the most fundamental feature of the repression of Black male slaves practiced by white men was the stripping them of masculine qualities. These practices included the usurpation of authority, as well as denying the ability to provide for one's family and the right to own property. In order to survive in the system that was racist and segregated to such a great degree, Black men began to rely ever more greatly on those areas of masculinity that were still available to them, such as physical strength, sexual prowess and staying in control. "The incorporation of a code of 'macho' behavior is thus intelligible as a means of recuperating some degree of power over the condition of powerlessness and dependency in relation to the white master subject," Mercer and Julien (1994, 137–138, cit. Hall 1997, 262) conclude. African-American men thus behave according to their stereotype because it provides them with the opportunity to be tough, which is absolutely necessary because they must constantly encounter racism or, at the very least, the danger of it.

When we analyze the visual orders of the poster, the textual part is also important. A poster is a multimodal presentation where written text is articulated into the picture's meanings. Here the text seamlessly supports the visual order of the "bad nigga," in which Blacks are represented, and represent themselves, as a threat to the status of the white race on the earth. The poster is also incorporated as part of youth culture which crosses ethnic borders. Even if someone did not like the Black rebellion represented by Public Enemy, s/he might still like the band's street credibility: it is uncompromising, genuine and aggressive—all central elements in rock mythology.

The poster wound up on my kitchen wall like this: on my way to work, I used to cut through the railway station, where the town's best poster shop was located at that time. I faced the gaze of the African-American men of Public Enemy many times before I finally stepped inside the shop. The poster sold itself to me by looking at me from the shop window and by evoking a fantasy about how good it would look on the wall of my flat. I was not interested in Public Enemy only because the band was visually impressive. I had also listened to their music and bought their records.

The poster thus becomes part of many visual orders, of which, as far as I could see, the "bad nigga" and the strong masculinity linked to it were most central. If I had felt antipathy towards the meanings of these visual orders, the poster would hardly have found its way to my wall. It was probably precisely these meanings that drew me to buy the poster. Now it is part of my kitchen's visual order and no longer a picture of African-American men only, it is also a picture of me. Through the visual orders of the picture I communicate a certain image of myself. The poster looks back at me and makes me contemplate the essence of its gaze.

My decision to buy the poster was influenced at least partly by identification with the masculinity of Public Enemy: the virile strength and rebellious nature linked to the band. Psychoanalytically examined, the superior masculinity is the ideal *ego* towards which many men continuously strive, but which they can never fully reach. In these terms, Black and White men can in fact share a common experience. The ideal of masculinity is a desirable state for both. On the other hand, Black and White men's relation to masculinity is asymmetrical due to their historical relationship with one another. Hyper-masculinity is not only a stereotype connected to the Black man; in fact it is the white man's fantasy of the Black man that emerges from a deep unconscious level and articulates with many other racial simplifications. One of these is the notion of the African-American man as child-like; treating him patronizingly like an uncivilized child, who is not quite responsible for his own deeds. According to Hall (1997, 263), this kind of a predisposition "may be a cover-up, for a deeper, more troubling fantasy (...) that Blacks are really super-men, better endowed than whites, and sexually insatiable." It would be inappropriate and racist to openly express the latter feeling, but nevertheless, the fantasy is there and many quietly accept it. When Blacks behave in a macho fashion, they impugn the stereotype (according to which they are children). Yet, at the same time, they reinforce the fantasy found behind the stereotype or which is constructed on its unconscious level (Blacks are aggressive, overly sexual and sexually too well-endowed). The Black man has indeed fallen in a kind of a double bind: as he breaks through one stereotype, he simultaneously reinforces another.

Hall's interpretation of the situation is that the Blacks have been caught in the trap of a stereotypical structure. They must shuttle between the two polar ends and at times they are presented as embodying both extremes at once: the African-American man is a little boy with an adult man's phallus. As far as I could see, the strategies of infantilizing the Black man were not present in the poster, unless young men's unilateral rebellion is considered childish. Had I come across infantilizing strategies, I would hardly have hanged the poster on my wall. Or, let's put it this way: I could identify with the masculine tension of the poster because it corresponds with the meanings that form a significant part of my ideal type of masculinity.

In addition to masculinity, the poster takes its place in my personal history and the visual order of my rooms also in a different way. When I was an 18-year-old youth, I had a poster of Che Guevara on my wall. In that picture—the handsome, bearded Che in camouflage—the meanings of masculinity and aggression were also very much on the surface. The guerrilla leader Che represented "justified violence," the struggle of Latin American countries to achieve a just society. By the means of its visual orders, the Public Enemy poster becomes part of the same revolutionary movement: the struggle for a fair world. This is the fantasy that the poster still feeds in my mind.

When I bought the poster, it was as if I had clad myself in it. Through the poster's visual orders, I prepared to meet the looks directed at me by hanging it on my wall. Adapting into visual orders, playing with them or resisting them is symbolic work, which, cultural studies researcher Paul Willis has discussed in his work, *Common Culture* (1990). Willis analyzes the youth cultures of British society, in which the youth perform symbolic work by confronting each other on the streets and through conversation. This building of identities—largely in the areas of consumption and leisure time—is, for Willis, a common culture that is juxtaposed with the high culture constructed within art institutions. Where artists are creative through their work exhibited in galleries, people are creative in their everyday activities, in their symbolic work. Willis (1990, 11) distinguishes four features in his study.

The first feature is language "as a practice and symbolic resource." According to Willis's views, language is the primary means for communication. It makes interaction and the sense of solidarity with others possible. Through the means of language, we are able to put ourselves in another person's place and, at the same time, understand ourselves as "the others." However, here Willis seems to forget the verbal and nonverbal dimension of identification. When we see a picture of a person who has suffered a loss, we can feel compassion even if we do not share common language with him/her.

The second feature (*ibid.*) has to do with corporality. "The body is the site of somatic knowledge as well as the set of signs and symbols. It is the source of productive and communicative activity—signing, symbolizing, feeling."

The third dimension of symbolic work is connected to the dramaturgy of interaction. Communication is not automatic; it does not happen via wires running between our heads. Communication always takes place in mutually produced roles, rituals and performances. "Dramaturgical components of the symbolic include a variety of non-verbal communications, as well as sensuous cultural practices and communal solidarities. These include dancing, singing, joke-making, story-telling in dynamic settings and through performance." (*Ibid.*)

The fourth dimension of symbolic work is, in fact, a kind of an umbrella concept for the three other ones, namely, language, corporality and dramatic forms. The question is one of producing new meanings on the basis of the three features. It is expressly here where human creativity rests. People can build new cultural meanings of already existing meanings either on their own or together, and by doing symbolic work they can open up new ways of experiencing and being. The most significant "product" of symbolic work is identity. As far as people can possibly construct their identities, symbolic work enables both the questioning of existing identities and the construction of new ones. Moreover, symbolic work positions identities into relation with one another and as part of a broader entity. In this sense, identities are historical; bound to time and place. A person cannot select an identity as s/he selects goods on the self of a shop. S/he is determined by his or her surroundings and culture. However, "locations and situations are not only *determinations*—they're also relations resources to be discovered, explored and experienced" (*ibid.*, 12). Hence it is not possible to learn ethnicity, class or social gender. One lives in these identities and tests their limits.

By purchasing the poster of Public Enemy I undeniably performed symbolic work, at least partially in the terms Willis discusses it. I continue to construct my own identity with the help of the poster because it forms a part of my personal space. What is amusing here is that my middle-aged superego both seduces and denies me, utilizing youthful imagery as the building blocks of my identity.

CHAPTER FOUR

READING PICTURES

S UNDAY MORNINGS WITH my eight-year-old daughter Siri usually follow more or less the same pattern: I wake up about seven, brew some coffee and read the morning papers in peace and quiet. A little later, Siri scrambles out of bed. She gives me a hug and we chat a little while she has her breakfast. Soon she leaves the table to watch children's programs on TV. I don't let Siri watch much TV on her own, and when I do, only children's programs are allowed. Every now and then we watch nature shows and Finnish TV series together. It is not insignificant to me how much time Siri spends in front of the TV. Like many other parents, I fear that TV steals a big chunk of her time which could be employed in a much more *useful* way, like reading books.

Apparently I have managed to make TV a problem that demands deep and multi-dimensional reflection.

Fortunately, I am not alone in my worries. Already at the end of the 1960s there was a general awakening with regard to how watching TV affects children. It appeared that learning difficulties among children beginning school had increased as watching TV became more common.[1]

This fact was among the reasons that drove calls to convene a conference on visual literacy in 1968. The participants came from many fields: there were language teachers, anthropologists, sociologists, photographers, artists. Around the same time, the International Visual Literacy Association (IVLA) was founded as a consortium for people who were interested in visual literacy (Debes 1986 in Pett 1988).

The concerns about children's literacy were therefore connected to the technological and cultural transition: the arrival of the TV in every family's living room. On the one hand, there was apprehension that technology, though seductive in many ways, extinguishes children's interest in reading. On the other hand, it was thought that the fresh and highly visual media can create new ways of literacy. It was believed that the development of visual literacy can provide children—perhaps even adults as well—with the means to become more detached from the world of the TV, or at least to watch it critically. It is easy to see that the current literacy discourse concerning digital technology and the Internet contains similar ingredients. The anxiety about literacy is linked with the threats, promises and demands brought about by the current technological and cultural transition.

The conference reports of the IVLA reveal how many different viewpoints there can be in perceiving visual literacy: psychologists, sociologists, artists, information technology professionals, graphic artists and teachers all speak of their own visions of visual literacy (see Griffin et al. 1999; 2000). Among others, the following topics can be found in the reports: graphic symbols—design and meaning; images—how much we recall; video technologies for the web; and creating effective visual metaphors. The articles are written from different points of departure and rarely refer to the same sources. When exploring the theoretical roots of visual literacy, works like Gyorgy Kepes's *Language of Vision*, Colin Turbayne's *Myth of Metaphor* and Rudolf Arnheim's *Art and Visual Perception* have been considered significant (Pett 1988). However, at the turn of the millennium, nobody writing conference publications appears to refer to these sources any longer. Today, visual literacy has been thematized from many different points of departure and disciplines. When the first conferences of the IVLA were organized, John Debes defined visual literacy in the following way:

> Visual literacy refers to a group of vision competencies a human being can develop by seeing and at the same time having and integrating other sensory experiences. The development of these competencies is fundamental to normal human learning. When developed, they enable a visually literate person to discriminate and interpret visual actions, objects and symbols natural or man-made, that he encounters in his environment. Through the creative use of these competencies, he is able to communicate with others. Through the appreciative use of these competencies, he is able to comprehend and enjoy the masterworks of visual communications. (Cit. Sinatra 1986, 55)

It follows from this definition that visual literacy is intrinsically linked with other sensory forms in addition to the development of perception. People naturally learn some aspects of visual literacy in everyday interaction; for instance, there is no need to learn to read the meanings of most nonverbal messages in the same way as written text. It is also possible to develop visual literacy in multiple ways and to learn to read cultural symbols in more subtle ways, as well as communicate through them. However, there is one important notion missing in the definition: in this book, visual literacy means reflection on the meanings of the visual word, as well as their *critical* analysis, rather than merely adapting to the prevailing visual orders.

I will not extensively explore this multidisciplinary field of visual literacy research here. I focus instead on the ideas of two researchers, Richard Sinatra and Paul Messaris. Sinatra discusses the relationship between visual literacy and verbal development, whereas Messaris examines the distinction between pictorial and non-pictorial perception. I explore some of their thoughts and discuss the relationship between these ideas and visual orders—a concept, by the way, which is not used by either one of the researchers.

VISUAL LITERACIES

According to Richard Sinatra (*ibid.*, 5), "visual literacy is the active reconstruction of past visual experience with incoming visual messages to obtain meaning." For example, the meanings of the "do not enter" traffic sign are always created on the basis of an earlier visual experience and connected to the specific meanings of each interpretive situation.

Two things can be highlighted in Sinatra's definition. First, Sinatra considers visual literacy an action that produces meanings. Secondly, because visual literacy is a meaning-producing activity, it is also linked to the formation of verbal meanings. Moreover, Sinatra thinks that as individuals develop, visual literacy precedes other stages of literacy. Before commanding language, a child learns to recognize visual forms, such as the face of his/her caregiver. Growing into language and visual literacy develop side by side, but it is reasonable to think that a child learns to recognize visual figures that are meaningful to him/her prior to signs of spoken or written language. In this sense, visual literacy precedes learning to speak.

Sinatra draws on the Swiss Jean Piaget's (1896–1980) developmental psychology studies. Since birth, a child is an assiduous explorer and observer who continuously learns by being in interaction with his/her surroundings. Children manipulate their environment and make observations of what is going on. On the basis of their experiences, children work on pre-verbal images and make mental schemes. In a pre-verbal stage, a child picks up what s/he learns largely from different visual and motoric stimuli where the eye converges with the movements of the body. Sinatra calls the ability to use and formulate schemes—through experimenting and looking—primary visual literacy. This is the foundation for literacies that develop later on. The skill to read non-verbal messages, which is first developed in early childhood, remains throughout adulthood and continuously acquires new

contents. Expressions, postures of the body, style of dress and appearance all communicate both within and outside language, as was shown earlier.

It is probably largely a matter of agreement whether perceptions of nonverbal
or pre-verbal messages can be called thinking. Nonverbal images have an effect on
us, for example, in the arena of identification: I can identify with a given quality
of a certain person without verbally articulating it at all. I can also identify with
a more or less abstract situational image. I can, for instance, drift off into a day
dream in which I relax alone on the beach of a paradise island and awaken to
reality only much later.

Through the means of images, a child conceives that a certain object exists
even though it is not immediately present. The image of the family dog is alive in
the mind of a child, even if the animal is nowhere to be seen at that moment. It is
important for the development of language that at the age of 2–6 years, schemes
begin to represent one another. In a child's play, a chunk of wood may be a deli-
cious meal, a cardboard box becomes a race car, a soft wad of fabric is a bunny
rabbit. This is when a sign begins to diverge from a concrete object to become a
part of the symbolic system of other signs, and at the same time, one of the central
features of verbal language. In fact this is the moment in a child's development
when representations begin to develop. This means that an object (later a picture
and a word) comes to represent and symbolize something external to it, an image.
"Language, then, becomes the natural extension of symbolic thought, and symbolic
thoughts help form the mental schemata of a visually literate person," Sinatra
(*ibid.*, 11) summarizes.

Growing into language is thus a visual process as well in which the eye plays
a central role. When my daughter was small and had not yet mastered language, I
often asked her: "do you want milk?" while showing her a milk carton. The visual
quality of language became even more apparent later when together we guessed
what different pictures might represent and mean.

Sinatra indeed calls, perhaps rather provocatively, the ability to use and understand language "our second literacy." When the above-described schemes become
separate from the meanings that are tied to objects and become bound to verbal
signs and the sign system they construct, a child gradually moves on to verbal
expressions. S/he learns to recognize the expression "dog" when the word is said
aloud while pointing to a real dog or a picture of a dog. Children learn verbal
expressions by attaching them to a nonverbal image.

In the early stages of verbal expression, children produce expressions which
represent thoughts connected to needs, or to satisfying those needs (*ibid.*, 15).
When s/he wants milk, a child at first says something like "ilk," then "want milk"

and finally "can I have milk." Verbal capacity expands in two directions. On the one hand, expressions become more complex and extensive; while on the other hand, a child learns to use the structure of the language more dexterously, to formulate correct speech with appropriate sentence elements. Naturally, all this occurs in interaction with other children and adults. A child always experiences language in situations where condensed emotions—joy, sorrow, anxiety and so on—have an impact on how strong engrams are depicted in the mind.

After learning oral literacy, that is, speaking and listening, a child moves on to the third stage of literacy which consists of traditional reading and writing. Sinatra calls this written literacy. He emphasizes that all three areas of literacy have an impact on one another. The development of written literacy also provides us with the tools of seeing. I can easily recall several texts that made me begin to look at pictorial culture with different eyes. Abigail Solomon-Godeau's writings have helped me learn to critically assess photographs as part of the art of photography; Roland Barthes has helped me to see myths in pictures; Kaja Silverman has made me think about how a picture looks back at the viewer. However, pictures have also raised challenges to texts and opened new viewpoints to them. Benetton's advertisements, in all their ambiguity, have made me evaluate the texts written about them with a critical eye. At their best, pictorial, nonverbal presentations have provided an impetus to their viewers to start a public discourse, and perhaps even to reassess written and pictorial tradition similar to the previously mentioned, *Ecce Homo* pictures by Elisabeth Ohlson, which excited a debate about interpretations of the Bible (see p. 42). Powerful pictures can thus coerce us to return to the fundamental texts of our culture and ask how they should be properly understood.

The fourth dimension of literacy is connected to pictorial culture, to the production and consumption of its representations. Sinatra (*ibid.*, 28) calls this form of visual literacy representational communication. It is characterized by imagining, production and aesthetic engagement. This dimension of visual literacy covers the areas of visual arts, media and aesthetics. Imagining and production refer to the receptive and expressive processes of this literacy.

Visual literacies do not form a hierarchy. Therefore, the means of presenting a film, for example, can interact directly with the basic elements of literacy, oral literacy or written literacy. The understanding that wells from each area of literacy enriches the functioning of the other areas throughout a person's entire lifetime.

Finally, Sinatra articulates his analysis with cerebral physiology. His text is therefore different from this book in terms of the points of departure. The starting points of this book are in cultural studies and the interpretation of meanings. Sinatra's four-part categorization of literacy is quite formulaic, which he admits himself. However, the categorization illustrates well how verbal and nonverbal literacy depend on one another. If primary visual literacy is essential for the development of oral and written literacy, it follows that processing and producing pictorial material in childhood create the preconditions for the maturation of lingual expression.

While the beginning of this book has concentrated on the development of a broader visual literacy in which different visual orders, the individual's position within them and the power of the Gaze play a major role, the end of this chapter and rest of the book emphasize the problematics of pictures—photographs in particular—with regard to visual literacy.

PICTURES AND VISUAL LITERACY

As far as I can see, Sinatra's categorization of literacies is in harmony with the core notion of this book: visual literacy can be defined as the ability to understand the cultural meanings of visual orders. Visual literacy also means the ability to conceive the historical quality of visual orders and the power processes connected with them as well as to distinguish alternative orders. Visual literacy is thus not only an understanding of the visible reality, but at its best it is also the production of such representations that challenge pictorial stereotypes connected, for instance, to the representation of race and gender. The Benetton advertisement picture, *Family of the Future*, below (Fig. 4.1) serves as an interesting and slightly controversial example.

Benetton utilizes ethnic groups in its advertising, and many researchers have criticized Benetton's campaigns on racism and racial stereotypes. According to Les

Figure 4.1 *The Benetton advertisement: Family of the Future.* © Copyright 1990 Benetton Group S.p.A. Photo: Oliviero Toscani.

Back and Vibeke Quaade (1993), Benetton turns the features of national cultures into stylistic differences between individuals, and thus fragments their national identity. The connections of the young people appearing in the advertisements to their ethnic groups disappear and are substituted with a kind of a play of differences which is then superficialized into style. Cultural differences are objectified into goods for sale. "The paradox demonstrated by the campaign is that the images of international communication and unity are realized by emphasizing difference and creating fetishistic images of nationalisms, crass racial stereotypes and images of otherness which are fragments and objectified", Back and Quaade (*ibid.*, 68) write. Therefore, Benetton's campaigns also maintain racial stereotypes and gendered myths. Back and Quaade (*ibid.*, 69) interpret the *Family of the Future* in the following way: "…in the absence of any naked male figure, the women and children are aligned to nature, and constructed as the locus of transcendental love. Race, femininity and childhood are articulated within a mutually reinforcing discourse, in which social constructions are naturalised by the association between women as nurturers and children as innocents."

The picture portrays two adults and a child. The black person in the picture becomes the central element in terms of interpretation. When the reception of the advertisement was surveyed, approximately one-half of the respondents recognized the person as a man, with the other half seeing a woman (Seppänen 2000). This interpretative ambivalence means that either a hetero- or homosexual relationship can form the core of the portrayed family. The representation therefore problematizes the notion of the heterosexual nuclear family by constructing a family form that consists of homosexuals of different ethnic groups who have adopted a child of Asian origin, a third ethnic group. This also became apparent when the reception of the picture was studied: people indeed interpreted the picture as a manifesto for multicultural families that cross traditional gender roles (*ibid.*). The reception of the *Family of the Future* clearly indicates that it is problematic to claim—as Back and Quaade do—that the advertisement maintains racial or gendered stereotypes. On the contrary, it seems that the advertisements, at least occasionally, affirm interpretations which work against these stereotypes.

Interpreting different pictures is part of visual literacy. However, it should be noted that pictorial genres do differ from one another. Interpreting a drawing differs from interpreting a photograph because there are not similar qualities or generic meanings in a drawing as there are in a photograph. Moreover, as I will later discuss, interpreting a photograph requires an understanding of nonverbal communication and non-pictorial visual orders. However, here I want to underline that *the distinction between a pictorial (mediated) and non-pictorial (not mediated) perception is analytical.* All visual perceptions are 'pictorial' in principle because a picture is depicted on the retina of the eye. This distinction is, nonetheless, necessary. It enables an analysis of the extent to which the interpretation of a picture depends on learning the interpretive codes of the medium. Should we learn to look at a photograph, or do we recognize the objects and people depicted in it in a similar way as in the not media-based reality? Does a photograph have its own language that we must learn?

In the following, I take a very close look at the photograph and raise some important issues connected to both the photograph and visual literacy. First, I discuss the digitalization of the photograph. The digital transition has brought up the old question of the truthfulness of the photograph. Many think that digitalization poses a threat to this truthfulness. Second, I take up the tangle of problematics entwined with the relationship between pictorial representation and the perception of its object. How does the perception of a picture differ from the perception of a reality that is not medium-based? Third, I consider the semiotic qualities of the photograph. I make comparisons between the photograph and written text and ask what kinds of semiotic qualities these two representative practices realize. I also introduce the semiotic functions that are central in terms of interpreting a photograph.

But why concentrate on the photograph? Is it not a genre of the pictorial that crumbles in this era of digital technologies? Focusing on the photograph is, however, well justified. First, a digital photograph is often interpreted through the same concepts as the traditional (analog) photograph. The history of the photograph is full of continuums, and its problematics, like the problem of the truthfulness of photograph, are still alive and kicking. The traditional photograph is also connected to many multimodal representations, such as the computer interface and different web presentations. It feels natural to think that *'photographic literacy' precedes web or digital literacy.* If one does not understand the functioning of the traditional photograph as representation, how is it possible to understand its meanings in multimodal interfaces and the visual orders articulated with them? The third reason to take up the photograph is its cultural value: it is still a very central part of everyday imagery from the pages of the newspaper to family albums.

DIGITALIZATION AND PHOTOGRAPHIC TRUTH

In the second chapter I discussed pictures people produce themselves and touched on the debate over the planned development project in a neighborhood, Vuores, on the outskirts of Tampere, Finland (see p. 51). Vuores activist Juha Suonpää's video was discussed as was his digitally constructed photograph that was published in the local newspaper *Aamulehti*. The photo represented Suonpää's vision of the future of Vuores. In the digitally manipulated picture, massive concrete blocks of flats were positioned near Suonpää's own home, an idyllic little homestead. A little later (7.2.1999) the same photograph was given publicity in a talk show aired by the Finnish Channel 4, to which Suonpää was invited. The Tampere deputy city manager lifted the photograph up in front of the TV cameras and claimed it was "a lie." He implied that Suonpää misled people with a digital picture that did not correspond with the planned physical reality. The notion reflected the thought, shared by many, that an honest and candid photograph portrays reality correctly. Thus, the sin Suonpää committed was not merely portraying reality mistakenly. His crime was much graver: he exploited people's trust in photographic truth in order to create an incorrect version of reality. There was an aggravating circumstance—as a photographer, Suonpää was well aware of how to delude people. It was as if a worker in the mint had manufactured counterfeit money.

A similar debate arose in connection with the Koskenniska Bridge plans, which I touched on in the second chapter. Many people who opposed the building of the bridge thought that it would clutter a time-honored and historically precious industrial milieu. The local movement that fought against the construction of the bridge appealed to the Finnish Parliamentary Ombudsman. The biggest Nordic newspaper *Helsingin Sanomat* published an article about the case on 13.10.1999. The article was illustrated with a digital picture submitted under a pseudonym. The picture depicted the bridge from the shore; it differed from the official pictures of the bridge published earlier and gave a remarkably clumsier impression of the construction. The truthfulness of this picture was also fiercely debated in public.

A discussion that raged in the Internet at the beginning of 2000 is a third example of the challenge that has emerged in connection with digitalization. The discussion concerned whether a photographer has the right to use an image processing program to fix a trace in a photograph left by a rain drop on the camera lens. The discussion, fuelled largely by professionals in photography, circled the same problem: what happens to the truthfulness of the photograph in the era of digital image processing?

In this discussion, strictly speaking, I am not interested whether a photograph is true or not, or when it is true, or whether a traditional photograph is truer than its digital cousin. I am more concerned with the problematics of photographic truth as such, as well as in the forces that influence its formation. From where does this problem emerge? Already in the 19th century, many considered whether a constructed photograph was true or not. Why does this problem continue to be processed century after century, moreover, with rather similar arguments? The question may be banal. People are simply and always utterly engaged in the contemplation of the truthfulness of different representations, be they pictorial or verbal, because they find it important or otherwise challenging. It may well be that the digitalization of the photograph generates a healthy reaction in people. Amidst all the digital tumult, the viewers of photographs begin to doubt the truthfulness of even traditional photograph more assiduously than before. We can no longer, and we do not have to, expect any reassuring truth effect from photographs—and yet, that is exactly what we expect, as the earlier examples show. It is precisely this paradox that makes the problem so fascinating.

Photographic truth can be connected to at least three things. First, there is the photograph itself. A photograph, or one of its qualities, can invite people to continuously contemplate its truthfulness. Secondly, there is the question of the positioning of the photograph in different practices. These practices can be such that they constantly raise the problem of photographic truth. The third vision concerns the camera. A camera is a machine. It can be such a simple technical device that even a child can use it. However, the camera carries cultural meanings and is historically intertwined with knowledge and knowing. How does the camera's cultural meaning affect the formation questions regarding a photograph's truthfulness?

It is most natural to start with the photograph itself, its ontology—or, to put it more simply, the "essence" of the photograph.

The Photograph

When the shutter of a camera opens, a kind of a material body is created momentarily. One end is formed by the target of the photograph; the other, by the film's light-sensitive coating or the surface of the (pixel) cell. They are connected by a bond formed by rays of light. When the shutter closes, the bond is broken. The light keeps on flowing, the target of the photograph continues its existence and the exposed negative or image data is multiplied into photographs which begin their circulation in culture. A photograph therefore not only represents its target, but is materially a part of it. The presence of a photograph is said to be similar to moon rocks, which not only represent but also are part of the moon. In this sense, a photograph is said to be a specific objective representation. In his *Camera Lucida* (1980), Ronald Barthes says that if a photograph is nothing else, at least it is a proof of the presence of the target at the very moment of taking the photograph. "In photography I can never deny *that the thing has been there*," he writes (Barthes 1993, 76). The objectivity of a photograph can indeed be considered part of its basic nature, as André Bazin notes in his famous essay "The Ontology of Photographic Image" (1945). A much-quoted part of the text deserves a moment of focus also here:

> Originality in photography as distinct from originality in painting lies in the essentially objective character of photography. For the first time, between originating object and its reproduction there intervenes only the instrumentality of a nonliving agent. For the first time an image of the world is formed automatically, without the creative invention of man. The personality of the photographer enters into the proceedings only in his selection of object to be photographed and the way of purpose he has in mind. Although the final result may reflect something of his personality, this does not play the same role as is played by that of the painter. All the arts are based on the presence of the man, only photography derives an advantage from his absence. Photography affects us like a phenomenon in nature, like a flower or a snowflake whose vegetable or earthly origins are an inseparable part of their beauty. (Bazin 1967, 13)

Bazin connects objectivity with the mechanical, automatic and nature-like qualities of photography. A photograph is born like a stone is honed smooth by streaming water or figures are etched on rock by a glacier: through sheer determinism. Because the "maker" of a photograph is nature, the photograph in itself is as infallible as nature, or in other words, beyond infallibility. Nature indeed can never fail or be defective: it just is. Bazin was not the first to conceive of the photograph as a genuine natural product. Even Louis Jacques Mandé Daguerre (1787–1851) himself, the developer of the early form of photograph, the daguerreotype, introduced his invention as follows: "The daguerreotype is not merely an instrument which serves to draw nature; on the contrary it is a chemical and physical process which gives her the power to reproduce herself" (Daguerre 1980, 13). The inventor of collotype, Henry Fox Talbot (1800–1877), bestowed his first book that contained photographs with the most telling title: *Pencil of Nature* (1843).

Even though Bazin emphasizes the nature-like quality of the photograph, he certainly does not refute the fact that the photograph is also the result of human activity by the photographer and therefore belongs to the sphere of culture. The photograph is thus split between nature and culture—counterpoints that reach far beyond the field of photography. In one form or another, the dualism nature/culture can also be found in the texts of other notable photography writers, such as John Berger or Susan Sontag. Moreover, it appears in many texts that concern the digital photograph, such as William J. Mitchell's book *The Reconfigured Eye* (1992). Mitchell (1992, 29–31) develops the idea of the photograph's *algorithmic* and *nonalgorithmic* character. Through these cumbersome-sounding concepts, Mitchell understands the above-described binary as a line. One end of the line is formed by the activity of the photographer, while the other consists of the automatic depiction of the image that is independent of the photographer. Mitchell (*ibid.*, 30) writes:

> A nonalgorithmic image, which is the product of many intentional acts, neither establishes that the object depicted exists nor (if that object does exist) provides much reliable evidence about it, but reveals a lot about what was in the artist's mind. An algorithmic image, which to large extent is automatically constructed from some sort of data about the object and which therefore involves fewer or even no intentional acts, gives away much less about the artist but provides more trustworthy evidence of what was out there in front of the imaging system. In between, there are images that are algorithmic to a degree.

A typical nonalgorithmic picture could be a sketch drawn freehand. If the drawer utilizes some sort of a technical device, such as a slide reflected on the drawing paper, the picture shifts towards the algorithmic. If a camera goes off unintentionally as it hangs from the neck, the depicted picture is strongly algorithmic. Mitchell seems to think that the more there is "intentionality"—human activity—in the picture, the less it has algorithmic extent and weight as evidence.

According to Mitchell, digital image production revolutionizes the rules of the game. It brings tools within the maker's reach with which it is possible to attach pictorial information coming from different sources to each other quickly and seamlessly. Moreover, this kind of image processing is very hard to detect. "The traditional origin narrative by which automatically captured shaded perspective images made to seem causal things of nature rather than products of human artifice (…) no longer has the power to convince us. The reference has come unstuck," Mitchell (*ibid.*, 31) writes. Digital image production makes it especially difficult to assess the algorithmic extent of a photograph.

Both Bazin and Mitchell examine the photograph here primarily through its technological foundation. Where Bazin perceives the photograph as nature-like and therefore objective, Mitchell sees digital technology as wrecking this objectivity and, at the same time, the natural quality of the photograph. In fact, here Mitchell takes the nature/culture binary that is at the core of the photograph and replaces it with the difference between the photograph and the digital image (see also Lister 1995; Manovich 1997). The digital photograph begins to represent the artificiality of culture; whereas the traditional (analog) photograph represents something more enduring, more natural. In this case, the nature/culture distinction begins to produce new distinctions, which in turn begin to appear in thinking that concerns the digital photograph. The most central distinctions are genuine/artificial and true/untrue. The composition hence created can be illustrated by the following figure (Fig. 4.2), which explains both fears of digital photograph and the cultural continuum of the problematics of photographic truth in digital image culture.

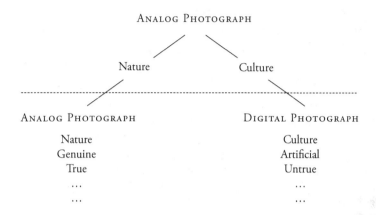

Figure 4.2 *Cultural distinctions in the analogical and the digital photograph.*

As a natural object, the photograph supports all those assumptions that wish to emphasize its objective nature independent of human agency. Yet, its factual dependence on a human agent constantly casts a shadow on its objectivity. This split in the photograph functions as a force that ceaselessly instigates questions about the truthfulness of a photograph, and—most importantly—penetrates thinking that concerns both traditional and digital photographs.

This shift is a beautiful example of the power of the nature/culture distinction and historical continuum. The analysis of the analogical era lives through the digital revolution and constructs a conception of photographic truth, which all of a sudden appears to be on the list of endangered species—as if the problem of truth was any simpler before. It is a fallacy which can easily be shaken by returning for a moment to about 150 years back in time; to the era when the photograph took its first baby steps in the service of different social practices.

Practices

In 1856, superintendent of the Female Department of the Surrey County Lunatic Asylum, Hugh Wells Diamond, gave a presentation entitled "On the Application of Photography to the Physiognomic and Mental Phenomena of Insanity." True to its name, the presentation concerned how photography could be applied to the treatment and diagnosis of mental illnesses. Diamond, who was also a founding member of the Royal Photographic Society, illustrated his presentation with photographs he had taken himself. He saw three tasks for clinical photography.

First, photographs can function as means of treatment because they have beneficial effects on patients. According to Diamond, patients examined photographs of themselves with great pleasure and interest; particularly those who showed signs of recovery from a grave dysfunction of mental activity (Tagg 1988, 78).

Secondly, photographs were records that doctors could use in their diagnoses:

> The Photographer secures with unerring accuracy the external phenomena of each passion, as the really certain indication of internal derangement, and exhibits to the eye the well-known sympathy which exists between the diseased brain and the organs and features of the body (...) The Photographer catches in a moment a permanent cloud, or the passing storm or sunshine of the soul, and thus enables the metaphysician to witness and trace out the connection between the visible and the invisible in one important branch of his researches into the Philosophy of the human mind. (*Ibid.*)

Photography freed the portrayal of the mentally ill from the prevalence of caricaturized drawings, which after the new invention became "nearly valueless." Diamond is among those who emphasize the nature-likeness of photographs with quite a grandiloquent emphasis: "The Photographer needs in many cases no aid from any language of his own, but prefers to listen, with the picture before him, to the silent but telling language of nature (...) the picture speaks for itself with the most marked precision and indicates the exact point which has been reached in the scale of unhappiness between the first sensation and its utmost height." (*Ibid.*)

The composition of the patient photographs resembled those of early police mug shots: a bare background, direct or nearly direct poses, a focus on the face. The angle of view in the photographs was influenced by the classification system of mental patients developed by Philip Pinelli as well as 18th century categorizations of patient pictures. The pictorial realization of patient photographs also drew from the tradition of portraiture in addition to hand-drawn catalogues of medicine and psychiatry, such as J.E.D. Esquirol's book *Des Maladies Mentales* (1838) and Sir Alexander Morrison's tome *Physiognomy of Mental Diseases*, which was published the same year. Diamond's photographic practices were thus born in a historical state in which the practices of psychiatry, physiognomy and photography, as well as science and aesthetics, were closely linked. An examination of Diamond's photographs shows how the photograph—only a few years after its invention—became an intersection to historically antecedent practices.

The third task Diamond set for clinical photography was the quick recognition of the cases. He writes: "It is well known that the portraits of those who are congregated in prisons for punishment have often times been of much value in recapturing some who have escaped (…) I have found the previous portrait of more value in calling to my mind the case and treatment, than any verbal description I may have placed on record" (cit. Tagg 1988, 80).

However, what does all this have to do with the truthfulness of the photograph? The problem can be considered with the aid of two concepts: documentation and the production of individuality.

In his work *Discipline and Punish*, Michel Foucault writes about how 'the individual' and the strategies of documentation began to intertwine in the 18th century. More and more detailed information was gathered about people in order to describe and recognize individuals easier. These methods were utilized to capture army deserters and diagnose cases in hospitals as well as for other purposes, such as determining pupils' capacities in educational institutions. According to Foucault (1977, 190):

> The hospitals of the eighteenth century, in particular, were great laboratories for scriptuary and documentary methods. The keeping of registers, their specification, their comparison during regular meetings of doctors and administrators, the transmission of their data to centralizing bodies (either at the hospital or at the central office of the poorhouses, the accountancy of diseases, cures, deaths, at the level of the hospital, a town or even of the nation as a whole formed an integral part of the process by which hospitals were subjected to the disciplinary regime.

The individual became the target of information, which itself obtained its own specific qualities. At the same time, a comparative system was created which made it possible to delineate overall phenomena, construct categories and negotiate an individual's positioning in different categories. Hence the methods of documentation made a 'case' out of the individual, which is simultaneously both the target of knowledge and the power linked to this knowledge. A well-known notion of Foucault's is that it is not primarily power that restricts an individual's scope of action, but power produces information and the realm of truth concerning an individual. "Truth is to be understood as a system of ordered procedures for the production, regulation, distribution, circulation and operation of statements. 'Truth' is linked in a circular relation with systems of power which produce and sustain it, and to effects of power which it includes and which extend it. A règime of truth," Foucault (1986, 133) summarizes, even if a little obscurely.

When a photograph is examined as part of these processes, the problematics of its truth extend quite far and the ontological viewpoint presented above loses some of its significance. The photograph is articulated as part of broader practices of power, which 'produced' individuality in the 19th century. The new invention was excellently suited to these purposes, and its use was not restricted to mental asylums only. Police began to photograph criminals as early as the 1840s. A little later on, the living conditions of the working class also became the target of documentation; "before and after" photographs became common in orphanages. Anthropology harnessed the photograph for its own purposes as well.

Certainly, the photograph had many utilitarian values in the 19th century. Calling cards, stereoscopic entertainments and pornographic pictures were central material for the pleasures of the eye. The photograph was attached to the construction of amusing spectacles at least as strongly as it was attached to the control and production of information about an individual. However, it became immediately clear after its invention that the photograph was being drafted into the service of visual orders that strived to determine the limits of true and appropriate knowledge about individuals through their methods and rituals. This had, and still has, two implications in terms of the truth of the photograph.

First, the new visual orders reinforced the photograph as a truthful representation because they tied the photograph to the production of information regarding an individual. This is easy to verify; all one has to do is take a look at one's passport or driver's license. The photographs in these documents link their object with quite complex systems of knowledge, the task of which is both the recognition of the individual as well as the attachment of certain facts to him/her, such as age, gender and citizenship.

Secondly, examining the institutional use of the photograph moves the problematics of the truthfulness of photograph beyond Bazinian ontology and on to practices of which the photograph is an intrinsic element. The truth of Diamond's patient photographs was first and foremost determined in relation to the psychiatry of the era and the categorizations of mental illnesses sustained in that era. In this connection, the photographs were 'true' representations of mental illnesses. The photograph has therefore never been an innocent, naturalistic representation of reality. It has always been intertwined with social practices and the struggles potentially developing within them. These struggles constantly entice us to return to the problematics of photographic truth, which time after time erupts into an open quarrel.

In 1936, the renowned documentarian Arthur Rothstein photographed a sunparched cow skull that lay on drought-ridden, parched soil. The simple set-up attempted to portray the agricultural crisis and harsh climate conditions of the American Dust Bowl which struggled in the grip of the Depression. Rothstein snapped many takes of the skull and shifted its place in order to create the desired impression. When the photographer's 'manipulative' activities were discovered, a debate flared up about photographic truth. Some politicians insisted that the nation had the right to see objectively truthful photographs instead of manipulated ones. In the background of the argument seethed a more wide-ranging political debate about President Roosevelt's New Deal policy. The debate over Rothstein's photograph was a tale of how conflicting definitions of social truth continually resurrect the problem of photographic truth. Had the photograph not been so fundamentally connected to the political passions of the era, which made the truthfulness of the photograph the crux of dispute, probably nobody would have paid much attention to the fact that the skull had been moved from its original position.

The Vuores neighborhood photograph by Juha Suonpää, discussed earlier in this chapter, has obvious connections with Rothstein's case. Suonpää constructed his picture digitally, whereas Rothstein staged the object of the photograph to suit his purposes. However, unlike Rothstein, Suonpää publicly stated that his photograph was an intentionally constructed representation. In light of what was discussed above, it could nevertheless be said that what is essential in Suonpää's photograph is not how precisely it depicted the distance between the concrete blocks of flats and his own little farm. The more important question lies in what kinds of *definitions of truth* the photograph is participating in and what forces raised the question of the truthfulness of the photograph.

When the Tampere deputy city manager characterized the photograph as a lie, naturally he could not have explicit knowledge of how well the photograph corresponded to the impending constructed reality that would come about sometime in the future when the development would be ready. Apparently, he had the drawings of the town plan in mind and formed his conception on their basis. His interpretation was also influenced by the fact that he had actively promoted the project and was very committed to it. On his side, Suonpää wanted to represent the feelings of dread that the project instilled in the residents of the area. To him, the truthfulness of the photograph was formed in relation to the planning process and the high-rise apartments he did not want looming over his home. Naturally, the larger question of who has the right, and under what preconditions, to determine visual orders was rippling in the background of the entire dispute. The controversy over photographic truth is but one element of the larger dispute.

As became apparent previously, the town planning officials had the means and tools of representation in their possession. They constructed different representations of what the neighborhood would probably look like. With his photograph, Suonpää broke this monopoly by producing a pictorial representation of the project himself. By doing this, he directly participated in the production of visual representations rather than being content to merely comment verbally on the sketches made by the officials. In the cases of both Vuores and the Koskenniska Bridge, the perspectives of the officials and the city residents were in conflict. No visual representation concerning these projects, be they digital or analogical, could avoid the visual orders constructed around the projects and the social power relations connected to them.

If the Koskenniska Bridge is photographed from below, the construction blocks out the entire sky. If it is photographed from an airplane, the bridge may look rather dainty. The very same photograph can depict either a spoiled rapids cityscape or a bridge prettily set within it, depending on the cultural context of the interpretation. With captions, the meanings can be further directed one way or another. It is quite futile to argue over the truthfulness of this kind of a photograph unless we simultaneously discuss the kinds of political, economic and social factors that are contained in the production and interpretation of any given visual order.

The Camera

In late autumn of 2000, an Internet discussion group was dissecting the question of whether a photographer is allowed to use an image processing program to fix a distortion in a photograph caused by a rain drop that hit the camera lens. What happens to photographic truth? The ridiculous-sounding problem is interesting because it shows the kind of a technical level on which the question of photographic truth most often occurs: on the concrete surface of a negative or a photograph. Hence, photographic truth is threatened by all those factors that prevent the depiction of the photographer's target by following the rules of optics as perfectly as possible. In this kind of analysis, attention is focused on the technical process, that is, the flawless working of the camera. Yet, it should be asked: could the camera have something to do with photographic truth also on other levels beyond the purely technical? This question is linked with the third factor that generates the problematics of photographic truth aside from the ontology of photograph and its social uses.

The relationship between the camera and the photograph appears so obvious that contemplating it seems senseless. A camera simply is an apparatus with which photographs are taken. However, the development of the photograph and the camera are not concurrent phenomena. The history of the camera began notably earlier than the invention of the photograph. Photographing is but one application of the camera, and most importantly: the principle of the camera remains alive and well in digital image production, in which a negative and the traditional print are no longer necessary. Moreover, historically, the camera is a larger phenomenon than the photograph in synchronic terms. As an image-producing technique, it extends from videos to small personal web cameras used together with computers.

The photograph thus forms only one application in the history of the camera which, in fact, is much more than the history of one technical device.

In the predecessor of the photographic camera, the camera obscura, light streams to a darkened room through a small hole (Fig. 4.3). An upside-down picture of the outside world is depicted on the opposite wall. Humans understood this phenomenon over 2000 years ago—Aristotle, for example, was well aware of the idea. The first actual devices were built in the 16th century and were used to examine solar eclipses and optical phenomena. At that time, the camera obscura was a room that people entered. It was also a magic place which produced mind-boggling performances in the eyes of the common folk. According to a contemporary observer (1652): "(...) charlatans have deluded some naïve and ignorant people by persuading them that what they saw was a manifestation of the occult science of astrology or of magic, and they had no difficulty in astonishing them and this afforded an opportunity to abuse the simpletons and draw whatever profit they could from this" (cit. Slater 1995b, 229).

The secular use of the camera obscura may have been by laymen, though this did not obstruct its rise to philosophical heights. Reflections on the significance of knowing and the possibility of definite knowledge marked reactions to the camera obscura. The camera obscura appears in the writings of many philosophers, such as John Locke (1632–1704), Gottfried Wilhelm Leibniz (1646–1716) and even Réne Descartes (1596–1650). In his book, *Techniques of the Observer* (1990), Jonathan

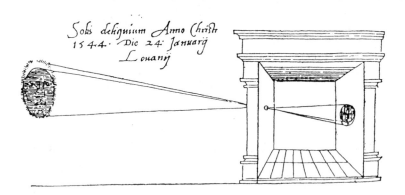

Figure 4.3 *A camera obscura from 1544.*

Crary describes how the camera obscura became the most common model with which it became possible to perceive both the process of seeing and the position of the knowing subject in the 17th and 18th centuries. He argues that nearly for two centuries the camera obscura served both rational and empirical philosophy as a model of how observation leads to different inferences of the world. The metaphor of the camera obscura is also found in a controversial part of *The German Ideology* (1846), written by Karl Marx (1818–1883) with Friedrich Engels (1820–1895), where it is used to describe how ideology functions. (Comp. Kofman 1998 and Haug 1984.)

The written histories of photography usually neglect its philosophical and cultural heritage and only depart from the perspective that it is a tool for making pictures which evolved from the primitive form of the basic photographic camera. However, according to Crary, the primary use of the camera obscura in the 18th century was not connected to drawing pictures. A 1753 *Encyclopédie* characterizes the device in the following way: "It throws great light on the nature of vision; it provides a very diverting spectacle, in that it presents images perfectly resembling their objects; it represents the colors and movements of objects better than any other sort of representation is able to do". Only briefly it is mentioned that "by means of this instrument someone who does not know how to draw is able nevertheless to draw with extreme accuracy" (cit. Crary 1990, 33).

Historically speaking, the camera obscura is a mechanical device, in which science, philosophy and magic are integrated. It revealed both the light of truth and the twilight of the unconscious. However, interest in the camera obscura collapsed after the introduction of photography. It had served its historic duty and was dismissed. The photograph smothered and continues to smother the camera with its cultural value and raw materialism. The camera became mere technology, a mere aid for creating photographs. Yet, what happened to the cultural metaphorics of the camera obscura in the era of the photograph? There is reason to assume that the appearance of the photographic camera and the photograph in society, as well as their entry in the sphere of consumption and recycling, provided new ingredients for metaphorics as well. Sigmund Freud, for example, used the metaphors of negative and positive rather than the camera obscura. According to Freud, all psychological phenomena travel through the unconscious (negative) before entering the sphere of the conscious (positive). (Kofman 1998) Later on, the camera raised discussion in the field of cinematic theory, where the spectator was seen to identify with the 'gaze' of the camera. The spectator thus takes the place of the camera and 'rules' the events on the screen. Among others, Christian Metz, Stephen Heath and Jean-Louis Baudry represent different variations of this

viewpoint. At the same time, cinematic theorists have emphasized the radical difference between the camera and the spectator, of which Jean-Louis Comolli is a
typical example (see e.g. Silverman 1996).

How do the camera's current cultural position and meanings affect the formation of the problematics of the photograph? What is the relationship between the
camera and the representations it produces in the digital era?

First, technologies connected to the camera are far-flung. Movies, videos, video-
phones and different surveillance appliances are based on camera technology. The
camera is thus a device which, mechanically speaking, is based on the eye but
simultaneously expands the area of the visible. The camera makes it possible to
examine a Martian landscape or the inside of the human heart. With a camera
it is possible to halt the flight of a bullet. The camera brings new areas into the
sphere of human experience and works like a prosthesis as it compensates for
the shortcomings of the eye. Moreover, because seeing in our culture is so very
strongly linked with knowing, the camera expands and reinforces our ability
to know (about seeing and knowing, see Jenks 1995). The camera has made it
possible to extend Bentham's panopticon outside the prison, as was noted in the
third chapter. When I enter a department store, I enter a sphere of camera surveillance. I can be unknowingly watched almost at any given moment. The camera
is therefore intimately linked in many ways with power and knowledge, visibility
and invisibility.

Secondly, the camera is and represents bona fide social power. Its presence
electrifies any given situation. A person who can effortlessly extemporize even
in a big crowd can become demure and self-conscious when a camera appears.
Similarly, just as we guard our words when taped, we become conscious of our
appearance when a camera is directed at us.

As I discussed in the previous chapter, in Jacques Lacan's thinking this was
connected to the construction of a subject in the area of the visual. To put it simply, it is a question of how being a subject is determined by the fact that we are
visible beings and exposed to the looks of others. The look of others does not have
to represent any form of concrete looking, but it can be awareness—conscious
or unconscious—of the fact that someone can see us. It is for that anonymous
gaze that we construct our outer appearance according to what we want to look
like in the eyes of others. This, in turn, is determined by cultural idealizations.
Hence, we process our being a subject under the scrutiny of the anonymous gaze,
always aware that we can at any moment be exposed to a real look that assesses
us. As a materialization of the gaze, the camera thus participates in the processing
of the truth about ourselves for ourselves. We are afraid that the camera reveals

our true being. The presence of a camera in a situation concretizes the power of this anonymous gaze. This becomes particularly clear in live television broadcasts, where the camera makes its object visible to perhaps millions of nameless eyes. From this perspective, it is not surprising that for Lacan (1977b, 106) the camera is a metaphor for the anonymous gaze. The photograph therefore lives in a cultural space formed by the camera. The camera expands our senses—that is, our ability to know—and functions at the same time as a real social power which makes the human objects of the camera process their identities in the charged space between the real and the ideal self.

The third field of meanings formed by the camera is connected to its role as a technical device. The camera is a mathematically precise scientific device, with which it is possible to slice an exactly determined piece of the world to be examined. The picture depicted before us follows the laws of optics and mathematics, in comparison to which our faltering sensory evidence is in fact a hindrance for getting a grip on true knowledge. The camera's closed, dark interior is a scientific laboratory where all intruding factors are eliminated. The picture is isolated for the mind to examine it. The traditional camera obscura also had this kind of significance. For instance, in Descartes's thinking, the camera obscura functions as a metaphor that makes up for the uncertainty of the senses. Crary condenses (1990, 48) Descartes's view of the camera obscura:

> If at the core of Descartes' method was the need to escape the uncertainties of mere human vision and the confusion of senses, the camera obscura is congruent with his quest to found human knowledge on a purely objective view of the world. The aperture of the camera obscura corresponds to a single, mathematically definable point, from which the world can be logically detected by a progressive accumulation and combination of signs. It is a device embodying man's position between God and the world. Founded on laws of nature (optics) but extrapolated to a plane outside of nature, the camera obscura provides a vantage point onto the world analogous to the eye of God. It is an infallible metaphysical eye more than it is a 'mechanical' eye. Sensory evidence was rejected in favor of the representations of the monocular apparatus, whose authenticity was beyond doubt.

The divide of the photograph into nature and culture, the photograph's positioning as part of social struggles of meaning, and the camera as a device that articulates with knowledge and knowing have a constant impact on when and in what way the question of photographic truth emerges.

When the digital photograph is interpreted as artificial and the traditional photograph as a more authentic representation, we are still moving within the thinking that surrounds the traditional photograph. The truth of the photograph is perceived on the basis of the traditional nature/culture polarization. This onto-logical split of the photograph can always, when needed, be mobilized as a vehicle for the rhetoric of photographic truth in different social struggles. The truth of both the digital and the traditional photograph is influenced by the social mean-ings connected to the camera, which extends from the historic role of the camera obscura to contemporary camera surveillance applications. When the digital and traditional photograph are juxtaposed, it is often forgotten that it is still the camera that remains behind *both* of them.

PICTORIAL AND NON-PICTORIAL PERCEPTION

One of the core questions of visual literacy is: do we apply some other codes or spe-cific rules of visual perception to a photograph than to non-pictorial reality? Does the photograph in itself not bear such a resemblance to reality that we recognize the objects of photographing as similar to other objects in our surroundings?

In his book *Visual "Literacy"* (1994), Paul Messaris confirms the problematic nature of the entire concept of visual literacy by relying on empirical research. He argues that the recognition of the objects of photographs, conceptualizing their spatial relationships, in addition to the narrative shifts created by juxtaposing photographs, are reliant on the everyday experiences of perceiving real objects and events. "The cognitive skills required for the interpretation of these aspects of meaning cannot, strictly speaking, be called a form of 'literacy,' if by this term we mean medium-specific interpretational expertise that can be acquired only through experience in that medium," Messaris (1994, 135) writes. He continues:

> What distinguishes images (including motion pictures) from language and from other modes of communication is the fact that images reproduce many of the informational cues that people make use of in their perception of physical and social reality. Our ability to infer what is represented in an image is based largely on this property, rather than on familiarity with arbitrary conventions (whereas the latter play a primary role in the inter-pretation of language, mathematics and so on). (*Ibid.*, 165)

> Unlike the conventions of written language or, for that matter, speech, pictorial conven-tions for the representations of objects and events are based on information-processing skills that a viewer can be assumed to possess even in the absence of any previous experi-ence with pictures. (*Ibid.*, 4)

Messaris largely repeats Ronald Barthes's well-known views, which hold that the photograph presents itself to people as "a message without a code." In his article "The Photographic Message," Barthes (1987, 17) writes:

> In order to move from reality to its photograph it is in no way necessary to divide up this reality into units and to constitute these units as signs, substantially different from the object they communicate; there is no necessity to set up a relay, that is to say a code, between the object and its image. Certainly the image is not the reality but at least it is its perfect *analogon* and it is exactly this analogical perfection which, to common sense, defines the photograph.

In other words, to put it in the terms used in this book: the photograph repeats the visual orders of immediate, not medium-based perceptions. This naturally has a direct connection with the problems of visual literacy and, in this case, photographic literacy. Is it worth speaking about photographic literacy in the first place, if understanding a photograph does not essentially differ from understanding the everyday world of objects?

Many basic textbooks on photography, however, tell us that viewers uniniti-ated in the photograph are not able to recognize even ordinary, everyday objects in it. The same story has been told by missionaries, explorers and anthropologists since the 19th century. Anthropologist Melville Herskovits's research provides us with a reasonably fresh example. Herskovits showed an African woman a photo-graph of her own son. The woman turned the picture around this way and that but could not see her son in it until Herskovits helped her recognize the familiar face. If these kinds of empirical observations are true, we can assume that it is necessary to *learn* to interpret a photograph. According to Messaris (*ibid.*, 60–61), there is no reason to doubt Herskovits's story. Instead it can be asked what the woman's problems in interpreting the picture tell us. She only needed a few brief clues in order to understand the picture. If there was some kind of a cultural interpretive code in the photograph itself, it would seem rather unlikely that that code could be adopted immediately by looking at just one photograph. Messaris argues that in many other similar situations photographs have opened up to viewers after only a brief introduction. There is also another common feature connected to these first encounters: in most cases, photographs have been shown to representatives of such cultures that have not been familiar even with paper. This effect of the photograph's material quality has been researched among the Ethiopian Me'en tribe. When members of the tribe were shown children's drawings printed on paper, they smelled, tasted and folded the paper but didn't pay much attention to the actual pictures. The experiment was repeated after the drawings were reprinted on cloth, which was more recognizable as a material among the tribal members. With this shift, the recognition percentage of the pictures rose remarkably.

It is obvious that the interpretative difficulties of people unfamiliar with the photograph in many reported cases have been caused by factors connected to the situation as well as the material qualities of the photograph rather than solely by the representational qualities of the pictures. The swift recognition of the photographs by the subjects after some brief guidance supports the assumption that the viewers apply the perceptive skills they already have to the pictures.

Messaris also considers one of the most common visual effects: by changing the angle of view, a person can be made to look either strong or weak. The trick works—with a few exceptions—both in films and in photographs: photographed from above, a person usually seems weak; from below, strong. Could this now be such a strong pictorial convention that the viewer can only interpret if s/he has learned to read pictures by looking at many of them? According to Messaris, this is not the case. The viewer can interpret these meanings via such an experience which has nothing to do with looking at pictures. The angles of view sum up real-life situations. One usually has to look up at a person who is stronger than one's self and down on someone who is weaker. Hence the photograph merely repeats non-pictorial visual orders. Messaris's argument seems sensible. The notion can be extended to include the nonverbal communication discussed earlier. Pictures repeat many forms of nonverbal communication, familiar from the everyday, which we have unwittingly grown accustomed to.

What specific feature of the photograph therefore demands literacy? We can also turn the question the other way: what barriers to understanding does the photograph set to its viewer as a form of representation in comparison to the direct observation of reality? Messaris raises three points which may cause difficulties for a viewer unfamiliar with pictures.[2]

First, photographs and pictures on the whole cannot perfectly duplicate colors and changes in light. A black-and-white picture obviously does not reproduce colors, that is, other than different shades of black and white. Secondly, a picture has to represent the three-dimensional world on a two-dimensional surface. Thirdly, many styles of creating a picture (shapes, stick figures, caricatures) eradicate a large part of the details of the object. This also occurs in photographs.

According to Messaris, it was not until studies emerged on visual perception, largely conducted by David Marr in the 1980s, that tools were created to deal with the above-mentioned questions. According to the studies, the transformation of the image depicted on the retina of the eye into visual perception consists of three stages.

In the first stage, information is transferred from the retina to the brain via the optic nerve. This information consists of fluctuations in the intensity of light and its wavelength (colors). Because the retina does not have the capacity to register the distance that the rays of light arrive from, the alternation of colors and intensity of light is two-dimensional, as is the picture depicted on the retina. It is the brain's task to process this picture into a three-dimensional sensation. The changes in the intensity of light can be caused by three factors, the first of which is the different intensities of light in the field of vision. For instance, sunlight can fall over different parts of the scene in varying intensity. Differences can also be caused by the diverse ways that the objects or their parts in the field of vision reflect light. The third reason is the discontinuity of geometric surfaces, such as between the object of looking, the background and other objects. (Messaris 1994, 47–50)

As an outcome of these processes a mental representation is produced, which roughly corresponds with a sort of outline drawing (primal sketch). In terms of perceiving pictures, the brain does not have much use for the two first-mentioned fluctuations in the intensity of light in order to create a three-dimensional sensation. In other words, to create a three-dimensional image, the brain uses mainly those alterations in the intensity of light that are caused by the discontinuations of the surfaces and the object the person is looking at. According to Messaris (*ibid.*, 50), it can be assumed on this basis that "…the absence of naturalistic light and color from a picture need not prevent the application of real-world interpretational processes to that picture. As long as the picture provides the viewer with satisfactory information about the geometry of the depicted scene, the real-world interpretational processes that handle such information can be brought into the play."

This brings Messaris (*ibid.*) to the next conclusion: "The notion that black-and-white photographs, monochrome watercolors, outline drawings, and so on, require special interpretational skills because of their lack of naturalistic color and/or shading is not supported by the work on vision cited above." The incomplete or non-existent capacity of a picture to duplicate colors and contrasts is therefore not a significant interpretational barrier to a person who is not used to understanding pictures.

In the second stage, the brain begins to discern depth. In other words, it calculates distances between the viewer and the perceived world of objects. This process of three-dimensionalization is an extremely complex process, but in terms of looking at pictures, it is possible to distinguish six central points in it (*ibid.*, 51–52):

- Binocular disparity. A slightly different picture is depicted on the retinas of the left and the right eye. This stereoscopic seeing has a strong impact on the emergence of three-dimensionality. It also has an important function in estimating distances.

- Motion parallax. Articles that are close seem to move faster than those further away, even if they move at the same speed.
- Occlusion. Articles that are closer to the viewer cover those that are further away.
- Texture gradients. If the perceived surface consists of regular figures, such as black-and-white tiles, the tiles furthest away seem to be more dense than those close to the viewer.
- Contours. The mere outline of some objects (e.g. people) can sometimes work as a source for a three-dimensional impression.
- Shading. Shadows on the surface can also function as a source for creating an impression of depth, although a very weak one.

Perceiving a picture's three-dimensionality is important in order to recognize the objects in it. However, a photograph lacks the two primary providers of the impression of depth: binocularity and motion parallax. This deficiency could be assumed to hinder the perception of a photograph's two-dimensional space as three-dimensional and, at the same time, the recognition of objects. According to Messaris, however, a visual perception is constructed in the brain in such a way that the impression or three-dimensionality does not necessarily demand the presence of all six factors. A person can thus apply only some of them to a picture and nevertheless understand that the picture depicts a three-dimensional space. S/he can indeed recognize the picture as a representation of reality by resorting to quite normal processes of direct perception.

In the third stage of visual perception, the viewer begins to recognize objects. Their central features emerge and the brain compares them to the engrams left by previous perceptions (*ibid.*, 13).

Recognition is based on the elimination of information. The photograph's deficient ability to reproduce the details of an object is thus a central mechanism of non-pictorial perception. In fact, the recognition of both pictorial and non-pictorial objects could be tricky if their perception was not based on elimination of sensations; discerning the essential from the unessential. If motion parallax and binocularity are not taken into account, perceiving a photograph and the non-pictorial reality appears to take place pretty much the same way.

Messaris intentionally treats the matter of perceiving pictures in terms of form. He does not touch on the cultural meanings connected to pictures but does (*ibid.*, 7) indeed remark that naturally familiar objects are more easily discerned in a picture than unfamiliar ones: "Although I do think that it is true that viewers get better at the interpretation of visual media as they acquire more experience with them, I also think that to a substantial degree the formal conventions typically encountered in still or motion pictures should make a good deal of sense even to a first-time viewer."

Towards the end of his book, Messaris says that visual literacy is above all the understanding of visual means. In practice, this means the capacity to see the special quality of a piece of art, for example, in the sense of the originality of its visual solutions. Visual literacy also includes the skill to understand the strategies of advertising which are devised in order to influence consumers. Here Messaris shifts away from the formal examination of pictures towards cultural meanings but leaves it at that.

Even though the perception of photographs and pictures in general largely repeats the regularities of non-pictorial perception, their cultural meanings are learned. Hence it does not actually matter very much whether we comply with the regularities of pictorial or non-pictorial perception when we perceive the signs of the photograph. Most important is how the matter represented by the photograph becomes meaningful as well as what visual orders it becomes a part of. It is entirely a different question—which Messaris does not deal with—that entire distinction between pictorial and non-pictorial representation is problematic because in our visual sensation we always perceive a picture. There are always two pictures depicted on the retinas of the eyes, from which the brain produces one whole, binocular picture.

Why, then, to differentiate between pictorial and non-pictorial perception? The differentiation is analytically important because it makes it possible to prove that *literacy of pictorial media requires the capacity to interpret the meanings of the everyday world of objects and nonverbal communication, such as the language of the face, gestures and body.* Visual literacy means the understanding of these often quite axiomatic and, at times, even unconscious messages; the cognition of their cultural meanings. Moreover, differentiating between pictorial and non-pictorial (non media-based) visual perception is important because *it enables us to examine the genre-typical ways of different media to construct meanings to the matters they represent.* The question is that which Marshall McLuhan refers to in his well-known remark: "The medium is the message." The common denominator of pictorial and non-pictorial perception is thus its *meaning*; through the meaning, the perceptions connect with different visual orders and lingual structures. One way to conceive of the means of the photograph to give meanings is to analyze the medium's semiotic qualities or functions.

SEMIOTIC FUNCTIONS

Semiotics is a science that studies signs, such as writing, symbols and pictures, from the perspective of the formation of meanings. The semiotic functions of photographs, which refer to how the photograph as a sign, or system of signs, conveys meanings, can be considered one of its means to become part of visual orders. Being familiar with semiotics is therefore important in this connection. Take a vase and a photograph of it. It is obvious that the vase and the photograph differ from one another in many ways. Nevertheless, we can recognize the vase from the photograph because the photograph realizes certain essential semiotic functions in regard to recognition, such as its iconicity. A photograph of a vase resembles a vase. Another example: I can not afford to purchase a genuine photograph by Man Ray for my wall. Instead, I can buy a poster of Man Ray's photograph. In this way, the photograph's iconic function enables me to construct the visual order of my apartment as I desire. The semiotic functions of a representation and the role of the representation in constructing a visual orders are thus tied to each other. Certainly I could try to draw a picture of Man Ray's photograph, but I would hardly hang that on my wall: in comparison to a drawing, the iconicity of a photograph is insurmountable.

If a representation's semiotic qualities are tied to the formation of visual orders, they are also tied to how these orders are read and interpreted. Even if I did not know the concept of iconic function, I would understand quite well that a poster of Man Ray's photograph is an exact copy of the original. If I am capable of understanding even the rudiments of what iconic function largely means, I can better apprehend the meaning formation of the picture and its ways of forming a visual order. In this case, semiotics helps us to understand the functioning of a certain representation as a part of visual orders. Semiotics attempts to provide us with concepts to better understand everyday meanings and perhaps to scrutinize them with a bit of detachment and distance.

One cumbersome quality of semiotic studies lies in the fact that different semioticians tend to define the same things by using different concepts and mean slightly different things with the same concepts. It is not a question of a marginal phenomenon, but it rings true even with the great names of semiotics. Let's think of one of the most fundamental notions, such as the concept of the 'sign' as defined by the American Charles S. Peirce (1839–1914) and French linguist Ferdinand de Saussure. The 'sign' of both of these semioticians can be illustrated with a triangle (Fiske 1990, 42–44).

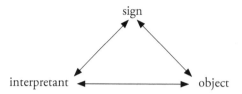

Figure 4.4 *The elements of the sign according to Peirce.*

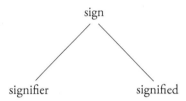

Figure 4.5 *The elements of the sign according to de Saussure.*

The tips of Peirce's triangle (Fig. 4.4) of the sign consist of the interpretant, the sign and the object, which are connected to each other by two-way arrows. The function of these arrows is to stress the fact that none of these terms can be understood as separate from the other two. The sign refers to the object outside of itself. The interpretant, in turn, is the mind of the user of the sign 'spoken to' by the sign. The interpretant is a difficult concept and should not be confused with the user of the sign. "It is a mental concept produced both by the sign and the user's experience of the object," John Fiske (1990, 43) summarizes.

De Saussure (1983) was first and foremost interested in the relationship of linguistic signs—chiefly spoken language—with one another. His 'sign' is constructed by the signifier and the signified (Fig. 4.5). The signifier is the physical being of the sign, for instance the word *car* written here. The signified is a kind of an immaterial concept to which the signifier refers to, namely, the idea of the car. In order for us to understand each other's speech or writing, we must understand the relationship between the signifier and the signified similarly; in other words, we must share at least partially the idea of a car.

Peirce's sign and de Saussure's signifier resemble one another, as do the interpretant and the signified (Fiske 1990, 44). Yet, they are positioned in completely different semiotic systems. Therefore, there is not only one semiotics but many different semiotics. In order to avoid confusion it is therefore always important to clearly define whether sign is referred to in its Saussurean of Peircean meaning. This is, however, rarely done in research that utilizes semiotics, and signs are generally referred to simply as signs.

The previously mentioned John Fiske (1990) has characterized the differences in Peircean and Saussurean semiotics in his book, *Introduction to Communication Studies*. At the same time, he has attempted to create a kind of user-friendly semiotics, where energy is spent in the analysis of everyday meanings rather than grueling terminological disputes. He has built bridges between different semiotic approaches and simultaneously concretized the processes of the formation of meanings. Fiske's book has indeed been well-worn in the hands of many of those interested in semiotics expressly for its clarity. As I go through some of the semiotic functions of the photograph in the following, I draw mainly from Fiske's thoughts and comment on and complete them occasionally. Fiske's clear conception serves the needs of this book quite well, in addition to being a good point of departure for semiotic examination. If reader needs a more thorough introduction to pictorial semiotics Göran Sonesson's *Pictorial Concepts* (1989) is an exhaustive introduction to the subject (see also Nöth 1995).

Indexicality

Of all the semiotic functions of the photograph, indexicality is perhaps the easiest to conceive. An indexical sign has a direct, real link to its object. Smoke is the index of fire and a runny nose is the index of a common cold. An indexical sign is often causal—a quality that can be summarized in the metaphorical saying "there is no smoke without fire." As the shutter of the camera opens, rays of light depict the object on the light-sensitive emulsion of film or the surface of the cell. Hence, there is always a causal connection between the picture that emerges and its object. In this sense, the sign is similar to the imprints left on the snow by a rabbit. Both fulfill the indexical sign's requirement of a direct link with the object. This is the first difference between the photograph and verbal language. The verbal language expression 'rabbit' does not necessarily have a direct link to any concrete rabbit. Where photographs are indexical, the signs of verbal language represent some given object completely external to them. They are not born causally through the interaction between the object and the sign.

Indexicality easily leads to the notion that the photograph is a solid piece of evidence that documents the existence of the objects it represents. This is, however, not necessarily true. There are numerous photographs of UFOs, but not many people believe that through the means of the photograph, the existence of flying saucers has been credibly verified. Thus, indexicality in itself is not a conclusive quality of the photograph, but when the photograph is linked with different practices and visual orders, it is easy to appeal to indexicality as if it was a guarantee of truth. Indexicality articulates with the struggles of photographic truth that were discussed above.

Iconicity

The connection between a photograph and its object is not only causal. The photograph is said to resemble the object. This quality is usually called iconicity. Verbal communication also lacks this semiotic quality with the exception of a few onomatopoetic expressions, such as the purring of a cat or a chirp of a bird. Verbal language is above all symbolic and the relationship between the sign and its referred object is contractual.

Semioticians, however, are not unanimous when it comes to the iconic quality of the photograph. Umberto Eco (1982, 32) thinks that there are always more differences than similarities between the photograph and the object it represents: "…from Peirce, through Morris, to the various positions of semiotics today, the iconic sign has cheerfully been spoken of as a sign of possessing some properties of the object represented. Now a simple phenomenological inspection of any representation, either a drawing or a photo, shows us that an image possesses none of the properties of the object represented." Cultural studies scholar Stuart Hall appears to share the same conception. According to Hall (1986, 132), a picture always turns the three-dimensional world into a two-dimensional representation. The question is of a complex semiotic problem, but it is rather fruitless to debate the notion that a photograph of, let's say a dog, resembles at least to some extent a physical dog more than the spoken or written word 'dog.' This is also suggested by the previously mentioned research findings which indicate that people recognize objects in a photograph at least partly in the same way they recognize the objects outside the photograph.

Motivation and Constraint

Iconicity also consists of the distinction between a motivated and constrained sign. A motivated sign is such that its physical being is bounded by the thing (the signified) it represents. The more iconic a sign, the more motivated it is. A photograph of a rabbit is more motivated than the word 'rabbit,' which does not resemble a rabbit in its appearance. A drawing of a rabbit is therefore more motivated than the word but somewhat more constrained than a photograph. The maker of a drawing can shape his/her object more freely—for instance, make the rabbit resemble a human being—whereas the possibilities of a photographer are notably more restricted. A photograph of a person is very motivated, because the look of a photograph is determined by the look of the person portrayed. There is reason to note here that when I refer to the photograph, I mean the traditional photograph which is not digitally manipulated. Through the means of digital image processing, the strongly motivated nature of the photograph, which is restricted to the features of its object, can naturally be weakened ad infinitum.

Paradigm and Syntagm

Paradigm and syntagm describe the two basic types of relationships between signs. A paradigm is a group of units of which only one unit can be selected at a time. The units must have something in common; in other words, they must have qualities that define them as members of expressly that very paradigm.

In order to form words, we must choose from the paradigm formed by letters, which contains a limited number of signs. Numbers, quotation marks and the exclamation point are not letters, but 'm' and 'j' are. In addition to common qualities, the units of a paradigm must be different enough to be distinct from each other. Selection is possible only by distinction. (It is exhausting to try and make out poor handwriting in which words and letters can hardly be distinguished from one another.) As a result of these paradigmatic choices, a syntagm emerges—such as a word or a sentence.

The angle of view is also a paradigmatic choice. A typical example is a camera directed at a person from below/up or above/down, which usually has an impact on the impression of strength that the viewer gets. Thus, all the angles of view used in photography form a paradigm of which the photographer selects the most fitting for a given situation. The angle of view, focal distance and shutter speed are fundamental paradigms connected to taking a photograph. Due to its iconic quality, a photograph is naturally just as paradigmatic as the object it represents: the hat of the person posing in the photograph is a choice from the paradigm of hats; the pair of trousers is a choice from the paradigm of pairs of trousers and the coat from the paradigm of coats. The syntagm of the outfit is the syntagm of the photograph. Moreover, a photograph itself is a syntagm: a choice from the paradigms of angle of view, focal distance and shutter speed.

In terms of these semiotic functions, the photograph is not as flexible as verbal language. Due to its indexicality, the paradigm and syntagm of the photograph are causally bound to the object it represents, which corresponding functions of verbal language are not.

Paradigmatic choices are connected to the visual orders that the photograph produces. It is a question of in what way the photographer chooses persons to be photographed from a group of people, or, rather, on what basis he chooses not to photograph the others. Are only photogenic people—often considered beautiful in the traditional sense—chosen, or does the photographer have mercy also on people that break the visual orders connected with beauty? Paradigmatic choices enable the reinforcement of certain meanings at the expense of others; they can either maintain or break the prevailing visual orders. All this is connected to the three following semiotic qualities of the photograph.

Denotation, Connotation, and Myth

Ronald Barthes brought the concepts of denotation and connotation into the research of photograph in the article "Rhetoric of the Image," which was published in the journal *Communications* in 1961. Afterwards Barthes changed his views many times and called the distinction artificial in his later studies. Nevertheless, the pair of concepts is perhaps the most utilized semiotic tool in photographic research.

Denotation refers to obvious meanings. The rabbit in the photograph is recognized as a rabbit. However, a rabbit is not merely a rabbit but also a disarming and soft creature. Connotations are formed of these "surpluses" of meanings. Connotation therefore arouses emotions, impressions and cultural meanings in the viewer of the photograph. The photographer can influence the connotations of a photograph by changing the camera angle or lighting, for example. Connotation is an important semiotic function because it carries *cultural values*. Through connotations of words and pictures it is possible to create different impressions of the same situation. "Pedestrian dies after being hit by a car" and "driver kills a pedestrian" give us two very different impressions. The paradigmatic choice of words often equals choice of connotations and, at the same time, emotional register.

Connotation is closely connected to the concept of myth. In primitive communities myths explained life and death, good and evil, the might of the forces of nature and godhood on the whole. Current myths are more connected to issues like the roles of men and women: through myths, the roles are anchored in place and become more or less obvious. According to Barthes, it is indeed the primary task of the myth to change what is historical to something that is natural, and myth's strongest characteristic is its obviousness. This also makes myth translucent, that is, hard to detect. In precisely in this sense, some visual orders are often very mythical, and it can be said without exaggeration that myth is one essential means of action in visual orders.

In one television commercial a father and his little daughter are flying a kite in a bucolic landscape. Suddenly the play is interrupted; the father realizes to his annoyance that his white shirt is stained. The girl takes his father's hand and leads him to a washing machine. It is her turn to teach daddy how to put clothes in the machine and measure out the detergent. At the end of the commercial the play continues, but the kite is replaced with the father's freshly washed shirt that is drying in the wind. The commercial plays with the myth that it is a woman's role to take care of men, and the role is learned from a very young age. The parallel myth is a small boy as the replacement of the father, the provider and protector of the family. I notice that I share the girl's joy when, for once, she is the one to teach her daddy something. At the same time, I am irked by the cheap pandering to the viewer with such an obvious myth. I am fairly certain that many viewers see nothing odd in the role models of the commercial; aren't they quite natural. In this respect the commercial, as many other visual representations, feeds the visual orders connected to the nuclear family. By the way, not a word is said in the commercial; the interaction of the actors is based on nonverbal messages and, naturally, music.

Advertisers react swiftly to cultural changes. While commercials maintain central social myths, such as the gender roles of the family, they also eagerly construct contradictory myths. As advertising reaches out to increasingly specific consumer groups, segments, it must also take into account those consumers whose lives break traditional gender roles. Commercials become open to more interpretations than the above-described detergent commercial.

Colors also participate in the construction of visual orders that forge gender roles. In our own culture, pink is connected with various feminine connotations indicating sweetness. Pink suggests emotional abundance as well as an irrational and fanciful relationship with reality. Pale blue, on the other hand, is more detached, cooler, and does not similarly catch the eye like pink—as if it were preparing a boy child to being more circumspect, detached and rational.

Metaphor and Metonym

Metaphors are often such a matter-of-course part of language and thinking that they escape closer scrutiny. People grind out text, recharge their batteries, get a load off their chests and paint the town red. They are beasts, bloodsuckers or build castles in the air. Every example reveals the central feature of a metaphor: a metaphor is a means to understand and experience one thing with the aid of another. There is usually no "load" on anyone's "chest." Hence the expression "get a load off one's chest" becomes an expression that functions as a tool for describing how telling about one's worries makes one feel better. In fact, the expression combines two metaphors. "Chest" refers to the person and "get a load off" to talking. The examples show also another important feature of a metaphor: it is always separate from its literal meaning. The "chest" in the expression does not mean the anatomical chest where lungs and the heart are located. The third quality of metaphor is its pictorial nature, which is revealed already by its synonym *figure of speech*. Figures of speech form an excellent example of how the visual articulates into verbal and vice versa. The well-known metaphor "to throw to the wolves" links something wolf-like, beastly to a human being, perhaps cruelty and aggression—all qualities that actually are linked to a wolf by humankind. At the same time, the metaphor invokes the visual being of a wolf, which is always more than the verbal description of the metaphor attains. The metaphor connects with many versatile representations of a wolf from the nasty beast in the Little Red Riding Hood to the natural species rambling in the woods.

A metaphor always contains two parts, the primary and the secondary subject. The wolf metaphor's primary subject is a human being and the secondary subject, naturally, is the wolf. Charles Forceville (1994, 3) has defined the notion rather cumbersomely: "The maker of a metaphorical statement selects, emphasizes, suppresses, and organizes features of the primary subject by applying to it statements isomorphic with the members of the secondary subject's implicative complex." These two subjects have an impact on one another in three different ways:

The presence of the primary subject:

- incites the listener to choose some qualities of the secondary subject.
- invites the listener to form a parallel implication complex, which coheres with the primary subject.
- induces parallel changes in the secondary subject.

The interaction between the primary and the secondary subject works also in visual representations. This can be illustrated by analyzing the structure of the advertisement of Benetton (Fig. 4.6). The advertisement is from 1990 and called *Condoms*. It shows a number of condoms of different colors that have been set in parallel to each other on white background.

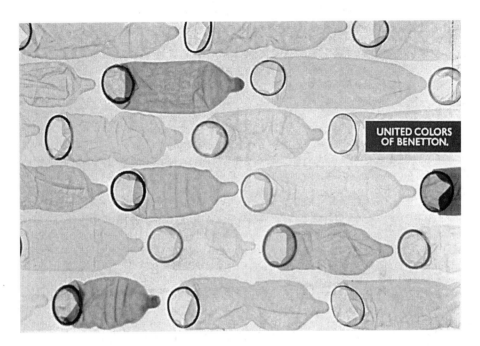

Figure 4.6 *The Benetton advertisement: Condoms.* © Copyright 1990 Benetton Group S.p.A. Photo: Oliviero Toscani.

The photograph is simplified and contains no other text but Benetton's logo. When I researched the reception of the picture, I noticed that many viewers see a marching group of people in the picture, which in turn is associated with a unified front and the struggle against AIDS. The condom has played a well-known role in this struggle. Moreover, some viewers interpreted the multi-colored condoms as a message that AIDS is a problem shared by all people, whatever color they may be. This immediately brings a new metaphorical dimension to the picture: condoms represent people of different colors. The same picture can hence contain several different metaphors depending on the viewer and the context of interpretation.

The core metaphor of Benetton's advertisement can be put in words: condoms are a marching crowd of people. The primary subject is thus formed of condoms and the secondary subject of a marching crowd. How did the viewers settle on this pictorial metaphor? The viewer of the picture is in a situation where the presence of the primary subject incites him/her to choose some qualities of the secondary subject. An obvious feature is the condoms displayed in the form of a marching crowd. A number of qualities are selected from the secondary subject: the question is not that of an army parade, but a systematic, well-organized march of people against

AIDS. At the same time, Forceville's third notion connected to the dynamics of the metaphor becomes true: the secondary subject changes because of the impact of the primary subject. In other words, condoms and their quite literal connection to the prevention of AIDS become the concrete manifesto of the marching group of people. The question is no longer that of an abstract picture of a march, but of a march promoting a very certain issue. All of these metaphorical shifts are influenced by the countless cultural meanings carried by AIDS.

In the interpretation of pictorial metaphors, context indeed has a decisive impact. Benetton was a familiar brand to all the viewers of the picture, and many were aware that the company has long campaigned against the spread of AIDS —to promote its sales. According to Forceville (*ibid.*, 26), there are at least three different contexts that can be seen in connection to pictorial metaphor: the pictorial, linguistic and cultural. Of the last-mentioned, he uses the expression "cultural knowledge". The pictorial context ties Benetton's picture to various earlier representations of condoms, such as condom advertisements, and marching crowds of people. The linguistic context is formed of Benetton's logo if nothing else, and the cultural context includes, among others, the discourse, fears and norms which define AIDS and Benetton as cultural phenomena. The metaphor would not work without these contextual factors.

Even though the photograph and verbal language both provide the possibility for metaphorical expressions, they construct their metaphors in different ways. One difference emerges from the linear quality of the expression. The verbal language metaphor, such as "a human being is a wolf," proceeds linearly from the primary subject to the secondary. In fact, this linear quality assists us to distinguish the subjects from each other: it is the wolf that lends something wolf-like to a human being and not vice versa. A photograph is a non-linear representation, and therefore there is no linear quality to help perceive the primary and secondary subject. The photographic metaphor of a wolf-like person can easily be confused with a representation of a human-like wolf. Hence the metaphorical context is crucial: is there a linguistic cue in the picture or does it otherwise belong to a context that underlines a human being's wolfishness?

Another difference between a pictorial and verbal metaphor is linked to the different semiotic qualities of the photograph and language. It is tricky to realize the verbal expression "a human being is like a wolf" through photographic means, unless the opportunities provided by image processing programs are exploited. This is due precisely to the fact that language enables paradigmatic shifts more efficiently than a photograph. Due to its indexicality, a photograph is almost bound to the thing it represents: a metaphorical picture emerges if the object of photography or the representative surroundings of the photograph provide the ingredients for it. We can easily imagine a situation where a courtroom judge's gavel has been replaced with a conductor's baton in a photograph, and the linguistic metaphor "a judge is like the conductor of an orchestra" is created. However, the realization of the idea is more complicated and may require the judge's consent to use of an image processing program. An example of the use of an intentionally rigid paradigmatic shift is an advertising campaign by Finland's biggest evening tabloid, *Ilta-Sanomat* (Fig. 4.7), in which heads of celebrities were combined with different bodies. The paradigms were therefore formed of heads and bodies.

Whereas meanings transfer from one level to another in a metaphor, they stay in the same level in a metonym. An example is the advertisement of the shipping company Viking Line which depicts only the letters NG LI (Fig. 4.8).

NG LI is a part that represents a larger entity. A photograph is also considered a metonymic sign because it always represents a part of a larger entity. Every aficionado of photography knows that by cropping the picture, it is possible to direct meanings in a desired direction. A close-up of a person's face gives a different impression than including the body would. In fact, the chosen metonymy often determines what kinds of meanings the photograph raises. Earlier the indexicality of the photograph was discussed, in the sense of its capacity to

Figure 4.7 *The largest evening tabloid in Finland,* Ilta-Sanomat, *combined the heads of celebrities with anonymous bodies in the campaign—an example of a paradigmatic shift. The advertisement's text in English: "You'll never know..."* © Copyright 2001 Ilta-Sanomat.

Figure 4.8 *The Nordic shipping company Viking Line uses the metonym (NG LI) from its name in advertising campaigns.* © Copyright Viking Line.

be materially—through causality—a part of its object. Through metonymy, a photograph is also indexical in another regard: it cuts a slice of a larger entity, and that slice thus begins to represent the very entity. These two indexical functions of the photograph function in different ways; only the latter is dependent on the photographer's choice. However, they both have an impact on the formation of the truth effects of the photograph and, through this, on what kinds of visual orders the photograph maintains and reinforces. For this reason, understanding the metonymic quality of the photograph is one of the central elements of visual literacy.

The photograph and written language thus appear to realize for the most part the same semiotic functions. The iconicity and indexicality, however, are qualities that verbal language (usually) lacks. From a semiotic viewpoint, it would indeed be important in teaching photographic literacy to concentrate on the analysis of the iconic, indexicality and metonymy. These semiotic functions are linked with much of the problematics of the truthfulness of the photograph and power, as became evident earlier.

Even though the photograph and verbal language realize the same semiotic functions, the functions do not work in the same way. The photograph can carry meanings in many regards and sometimes even better than verbal language, but its narrative arsenal lacks many central functions that verbal language possesses. A speaker can tell about the state of affairs as they were in the past, are in the present and will be in the future; as tangible things or in the abstract; as existing or conditional. In addition to these things, the photograph does not possess tenses or finite forms, the capacity to mark citations, non-finite clauses, proper nouns, inflections or fillers-in.

PONDERING MEANINGS

The development of visual literacy begins when a child perceives his/her environment and connects meanings to what s/he sees. The caregiver's smile is perhaps the very first nonverbal message that the child must learn to interpret. At the same time, the child begins to grow into a part of visual orders. Language and visual literacy develop side by side, and they cannot be separated from each other even later. A child quickly learns the visual orders of his/her living environment, whether they connected to non-verbal communication, the everyday world of objects and/or different forms of the pictorial. In this regard, visual literacy equals adapting into everyday visual orders, adopting their meanings and having the ability to function relying on established meanings. Visual literacy is therefore learned unnoticeably and, in a way, unofficially. People can watch television and look at pictures; we do not have to pass special courses to know how to do so, but if that were all there is to visual literacy then there would be no the need to write books like the one you are holding.

We can only talk about actual visual literacy when the viewer begins to ponder the meanings of representations and visual orders and becomes aware of the forces, structures and power relations connected to them. Hence visual literacy is no longer mere adaptation into prevailing visual orders but their critical analysis and questioning of the self-evident. This is valid also in contemporary digitalized culture. There is no shortcut to understanding the pictorial quality of digital culture, and, in that regard, to developing *digital literacy*. One paradox of visual literacy may well be that it can be learned only in a limited way by perceiving the visual reality. The best textbooks on visual literacy indeed analyze the entire society and its central meanings with insight, without concentrating on mere visual representations.

AFTERWORD

ISUAL ORDERS CONTAIN values and attitudes—they can be seen as embodying cultural meanings on the whole. They have an impact on every person's development as well as linguistic orders. Visual orders also resemble linguistic orders in the sense that it is relatively difficult to influence either one of them. However, even they are not altogether inflexible. At the beginning of the book, I introduced a photographic project called *All about My Curves*, which critiques the biased image of women in advertisements, as youthful beauty. This book includes many other concrete examples.

Even though one may not feel the urge to shake these orders, it is useful to learn to recognize them for at least two reasons. First, the ability to act and self-awareness grow when we are able to understand and analyze the meanings and flow of representations connected to visual interaction. The recognition of the power of the look and the Gaze, as well as visual orders, opens up the possibility to resist coercive looks, play ironic games or interpret visual representations differently.

When I dressed up as a woman and went to a very straight restaurant, I moved on the border of my own sexual and gender identity. I played games with my visibility. At the same time, I stepped outside of a secure visual order by breaking the dress norms of both the restaurant and myself. The performance led me to face both the pleasure and the insecurity that emerged from the experience. The scrutiny of the visual orders that are connected to one's own identity often demands introspection, the recognition of reactions and figuring out their meanings. This kind of scrutiny may be trying because it forces one to encounter his/her own limits and incompleteness. Testing one's limits, however, can also be light experimentation spiced up with self-irony.

The experience gave me knowledge that was somehow unstructured and not describable through language. Perhaps it could be termed bodily knowledge. It is condensed in sensations, echoes and the encounters of looks. This knowledge is valuable, even though it does not easily translate into verbal expression. Perhaps it is valuable precisely for this reason: bodily knowledge evades definitions and analytical scrutiny. The recognition and acknowledgment of this kind of knowledge are also an essential part of visual literacy. Is it not expressly one's body that becomes part of visual orders, which make it appear openly at one time only to disappear into the safe mass of uniforms at the next moment? Meeting the looks of others often demands conquering shame, which is an important step towards achieving bodily integrity. On the other hand, merely hanging on to the looks of others and acting solely on their terms can make anyone get lost in the labyrinth of identifications.

The examination of one's own visibility, relationship to images and identity is not far from self-analysis in which the borders of the ego are explored. Different psychoanalytical viewpoints have held a strong position in research on visual culture already in the 1960s. However, self-analysis has largely been bypassed even though the subject's relationship with the pictorial has been discussed from many points of departure.

In her article, "On Self-Analysis", Gertrude Ticho (1967) examines psychoanalysts who have had experience of self-analysis. Her research is thus limited to persons who have been through psychoanalysis. Yet, there is nothing that prevents separating Ticho's perceptions of this context and extending them into a little broader realm. This can be argued by the fact that neither Sigmund Freud nor Ticho think that self-analysis should be confused with actual analysis. It indeed lacks the mechanisms of transference between the patient and analyst that are very central in psychoanalysis.

According to Ticho, self-analysis requires a free flow of associations, and as objective listening and interpretation of the self as possible (*ibid.*, 310–311). Self-analysis also necessitates certain qualities in the person engaged in it. One of the most important requirements is a superego which is not too punishing, nor too corrupt or self-indulgent. According to Freud, a human psyche is composed of three areas: the conscious self (*Ich*), the unconscious realm of instinct (*Es*) and the superego (*Über-Ich*), which at all times strives to regulate the associations welling from the unconscious. The superego is at work, for example, when a person feels guilt for peeping or is shamed for being dressed inappropriately for the occasion. The superego also punishes the individual for 'wrong' thoughts, the exploration of which could actually be quite useful in terms of self-awareness. In other words, a human being who seeks immediate gratification in his/her life and strives to—perhaps quite wisely—avoid constantly impugning him/herself, is not necessarily the most fertile soil for self-analysis. This kind of a person often cannot tolerate anxiety. On the other hand, a person who is relentlessly harsh on him/herself and feels guilty for every insignificant incident in life is just as unsuitable for self-analysis. Ticho (*ibid.*, 313) summarizes: "The person who cannot accept and experience the grace, joy and light hearted humor of his infantile tendencies, but who expects predominantly dangerous and awful discoveries is a bad prospect for self-analysis."

Therefore, one must stop and take time in front of visual representations. One must understand that the seeing can continue long after the object of the look has faded from the retina. Visual literacy can be practiced quite well by reminiscing about images from years past and thinking about why it is these particular pictures that have continued living in my mind. What do I remember from them and why do I remember precisely that? Have I perhaps forgotten something? At times it is fairly easy to recognize one's own limits, for instance when pictorial material appears that arouses powerful rejection. The question goes then: Why are my limits set expressly here, from what kinds of issues does my rejection emerge? Why do I not want to look even though I do want to look?

Learning visual literacy does not always necessitate raking over the unconscious. It can be quite useful, though, at least when we are dealing with such visual orders that function in the areas of gender, sexuality or, say, ethnic otherness. It is, nevertheless, not worth getting embroiled into every interpretation. Moreover, not all visual orders are psychologically charged emotional explosives. There are a fair amount of relatively neutral representations from which one can pick out a lot of important meanings by casting an analytical look at them.

The semiotic functions described above can be used as tools of these interpretations. If the case is of interpreting a picture, we can ask: What kinds of visual orders are embedded in this representation and how are they constructed semiotically? Semiotics reveals the mechanics of meaning formation, gives names to the ways in which representations make things meaningful. Yet, it is also possible to penetrate to the core of meanings without semiotics by the means of cultural theoretical literature and research, as well as one's own experience. When I earlier analyzed the role of the Public Enemy poster as part of my home's visual order, I hardly used any semiotic tools. Instead, there were elements of both ethnic and gender research and my own experiences evident in the analysis.

Visual literacy in terms of its essential parts is indeed the capacity to perceive the visible reality as part of broader cultural structures of meanings. *With regard to visual literacy, the most essential thing thus is the understanding of the mechanisms of culture and the meaning production in society.* Visual literacy means challenging prevailing cultural axioms and seeing meanings where meanings are the least visible.

Visual literacy is—slightly paradoxically—the making of the invisible visible and known.

This book began its journey from the concepts of *visual order* and the *Gaze/look* and ended with the introduction of a few basic concepts of semiotics. The structure of the book reflects the order which can also be followed in studying visual literacy. Before what is seen can be understood, it must be understood how the seen—such as a pictorial representation—is set in different visual orders and how the Gaze/look and looking affect and form a part of the process of seeing. Visual orders and the Gaze/look have always been basic elements of social reality and human interaction; historical eras and cultural change, however, constantly inject them with new contents and meanings. Therefore, the central parts of the research and teaching of visual literacy are the exploration and teaching of cultural meanings.

Schools have a central role in the development of visual literacy. Students should be enticed to contemplate their identities amidst looks and visual orders. They could be encouraged to think about the pictorial that is important to them. However, they should just as well be made to stop before pictures that are seemingly self-evident and boring on the surface.

Len Masterman (1985, 13), the pioneer of media education, wrote before the breakthrough of information technology: "Schools continue to be dominated by print. To have difficulties in decoding prints is, in school terms, to be a failure. Outside the school the most influential and widely disseminated modes of communication are visual. (…) Schools, sooner or later, will have to recognize the importance of developing their pupils the ability to examine visual images critically."

Savoring Masterman's words brings to mind the cliché-ish, yet often so true saying: *nihil novi sub sole*, there is nothing new under the sun.

NOTES

CHAPTER 1—INTRODUCTION

1. The notion of functional literacy can be located in W.S. Gray's work *The Teaching of Reading and Writing* (1956). A human being is considered functionally literate, if s/he can efficiently participate in such activities of his/her own group or culture that require literacy. (See Barton 1994, 193; on critiques of the concept see e.g. Winterowd 1989, 4–7; Verhoeven 1994.)

   In the summer of 1987, E.D. Hirsch Jr.'s work, *Cultural Literacy* was published. The book began the discourse on cultural literacy that has been continued until today (Hirsch 1988 et al., xi). To Hirsch, cultural literacy chiefly means all-round education. The reader of a text must be aware of the same things as its author. This forms a kind of a cultural standard, a list of things which people should know in order to read texts properly and to keep up with the activities of the society (Hirsch 1988 et al., xii.; on critiques of the concept, see e.g. Winterowd 1989).

   According to Paul Gilster (1997, 1), digital literacy refers to the capacity to understand and use information in many formats by way of computers. Digital literacy is composed of, for instance, the skill to evaluate the information available in information networks. This requires a critical relationship to the contents of information networks, as well as the skill to piece together information found in different sources. (Gilster 1997, 2–3; see also Burbules 1998) The concept of digital literacy is also connected to cultural change, which is well illustrated by the name of Ilana Snyder's book, *Page to Screen* (1988). Texts are no longer read on the pages of the traditional book form but on the screen of a computer.

2. Raymond Chandler: *The Big Sleep*. London: Hamish Hamilton 1977, p. 7.

CHAPTER 2—LIVING IN VISUAL ORDERS

1. If the reader is familiar with the traditions of psychoanalysis or discourse analysis, the concept of visual order may ring a bell. One central concept of psychoanalyst Jacques Lacan is *symbolic order*, which refers for instance to how people are positioned as part of language; how they become linguistic subjects (See Lacan 1977a). In this book, I bypass possible connections between symbolic and visual order. Instead, I employ some elements of Lacan's concepts of Gaze and screen (*écran*) in the next chapter.

Besides symbolic order, discursive order—or, put more succinctly, discourse order—may come to mind. This concept, in turn, draws from Michel Foucault's thoughts about discourse and discursive formation (Foucault 1989, 31–49). They crystallize into the concept of discourse order within the domain of critical linguistics (Fairclough 1995, 55–56, 62–68). As he gives a definition to discourse, Fairclough (1995, 54) writes: "Like many linguists, I shall use 'discourse' to refer to spoken or written language use, though I want to extend it to include other types of semiotic activity (i.e. activity which produces meanings), such as visual images (photography, film, video, diagrams) and non-verbal communication (e.g. gestures)". Fairclough's notion is that visual representations can also be considered discourses, and he is probably right. Moreover, discourse analysis has become legitimate part of the analysis of visual images in some textbooks (see, e.g., Rose 2001). One possibility to process the concept of visual order would indeed have been the construction of an analogy between that and the concept of discourse order. However, that would have required quite arduous work and, as I made an attempt towards it, I found myself beleaguered by nonsensical theoretical fouls and a contrived end result. Hence, I settled for keeping the concept of visual order separate from the concept of discourse order, although they overlap in many ways. Additionally, I did not find it satisfactory to see an analysis of visual reality as simply an extension of linguistic discourse analysis. Visual representations frequently convey their meanings non-verbally as well (see next chapter).

While the concept of visual order refers to very concrete features of visible reality, it is also a theoretical abstraction which makes it possible to interpret visible reality and discuss it. I wished to develop a concept which is a fit tool for the analysis of all visual reality rather than only cinema, photography, art of painting or any other strictly bound genre.

2. Gunther Kress and Theo van Leeuwen (1996, 183) succinctly define multimodality: it is a text, the meanings of which are realized per more than one semiotic code. By text they refer to more than just writing. A photograph, for instance, can be a text.

However, the concept of code can be quite cumbersome. Written language consists of letters and a number of punctuation marks. They form words that in turn are arranged into a chain; indeed like the text at hand. The graphic format of a text has an effect on how the text is understood. Too small or too odd a font turns off some readers for sure; it is also not unimportant how the text is arranged into columns. People are accustomed to read established graphic packages. For instance, readers object to a too radical reform of the appearance of their daily paper, which happened to the largest Finnish daily *Helsingin Sanomat* in 1999. For many poets it is of utmost importance how the text is organized into a graphic whole. Yet, notwithstanding these issues it can be generalized that "the articulation of letters and punctuation marks, as well as the spaces that separate them, is not regulated by their visual attractiveness but the linguistic code which sets limits to the graphic modification of the text on the basis of the limited number of 29 units and the syntactic, semantic and text-linguistic preconditions of well-proportionedness", as Kalanti (1990, 16) writes.

If basic literacy expressly means the skill to decode text and meanings connected to it, one must be in command of the linguistic code described above. The existence of this kind of a code becomes even clearer when we consider the fact that it must be learned through toils and tears, as every Finn remembers from the catechetical meeting of the *Seven Brothers*.

Does a photograph, then, have a corresponding "language of the photograph" or a code that one must master in order to be able to interpret photographs? In these terms, photographs are not like written text. Everyone learns to look at photographs without difficulty in comparison to what kind of exertion learning to read demands.

Ronald Barthes was famously of the opinion that a photograph is a codeless message and an analogon, imitation, of reality. According to Kress and van Leeuwen (1996), this kind of a code does exist, a picture (photograph) has its own visual grammar that is analogical to linguistic grammar. Even though this kind of an analogy does exist, it does not mean that visual and linguistic meanings are created in a similar way. "Visual structures realize meanings as linguistic structures do also, and thereby point to different interpretations of experience and different forms of social interaction. The meanings which can be realized in language and in visual communication overlap in part, that is, some things can be expressed both visually and verbally; and in part they diverge—some things can be 'said' only visually, others only verbally. But even when something can be 'said' both visually and verbally the way in which it will be said is different" (*ibid.*, 2). The codedness or codedlessness of a photograph is linked to the problem of the relationship between pictorial and non-pictorial perception. At this I take a closer look in the fourth chapter.

3. *Helsingin Sanomat* 26.4.2000.

4. All references to Plato's texts are from the Project Gutenberg. Plato: *The Republic,* translated by Benjamin Jowett. Project Gutenberg http://www.gutenberg.org/dirs/etext98/repub11.txt, consulted 3/22/2006. Plato: *Timaeus,* translated by Benjamin Jowett. Project Gutenberg http://www.gutenberg.org/dirs/etext98/tmeus11.txt, consulted 3/22/2006.

5. Baudrillard does not clearly separate the concepts of simulation and simulacrum from each other. He often uses them as synonyms, yet occasionally with slightly different meanings.

6. It must be asked to what extent simulation and hyperreal are phenomena of the visual. Baudrillard's theorizing indicates that the social processes he characterizes are comprehensive and concern all social production of meaning, that is, representation in general. Since simulation and hyperreal concern all systems of production of meaning, it logically follows that also visual and pictorial orders are part of its domain. Baudrillard also places much weight on television and other visual media. In sensory terms, simulation and hyperreal are first and foremost connected to the sphere of the eye and are hence concepts that belong to the domain of visual orders.

7. Community photographing is connected to both the documentaristic nature of photography and the histories of different alternative communities in the British Isles. In more detail, see Braden 1983.

8. If we consider the opportunities photography provides for exploring and processing one's own identity, one of the most challenging authors is doubtlessly British Jo Spence. Spence's posthumously published *Cultural Sniping: The Art of Transgression* (1995), a collection of photographs and writings, is a good starting point to become familiar with his practices of photography. Spence has re-processed his own family album, photographed his experiences as a cancer patient and, together with Rosy Martin, developed a practice he calls photographic therapy. Spence's pictures startle and arouse rejection—hence, the subtitle *The Art of Transgression* is so very apt. Spence's habit of taking pictorial command of himself and his environment is bewildering. It means experiencing the limits of the unconscious, one's own deficient body and social otherness. Moreover, Spence's photographic projects inevitably bring up the question of how far it is necessary—and on the whole, wise—to test the boundaries of one's own identity.

CHAPTER 3—THE EYE, LOOKING AND THE GAZE

1. In German, the face and the sense of sight are expressed with the same noun *das Gesicht*. The German language also has the metaphor *das Gesicht verlieren,* to lose face.

2. Jacques Lacan uses one term, *le regard*. The English translation uses two terms, *gaze* and *look*, which in my understanding attain meanings that Lacan has given to *le regard*. Look refers to active *looking at* the object, whereas gaze is an *impersonal gaze that is directed to a subject*, and resembles Sartre's look of the Other. In this book, I use the term the Gaze when I refer to the latter. In spite of their similarities, Sartre's and Lacan's conceptions of the look and the gaze differ in many parts (see Silverman 1996, 167).

3. Jacques Lacan did not write the texts of his 'seminars'. They were edited on the basis of the lectures by Jacques-Alain Miller, Lacan's son-in-law. David Macey, who wrote the critical Lacan monograph, claims that Miller is just as much the author of the texts of the 'seminars' as Lacan (Macey 1988, 7–8).

4. *Écran* is translated into English with the term *screen*. Lacan characterizes *écran* as opaque. The term opaque can also be used to describe a glass plane or a drape that lets some light through it but halts the look on its surface. The light may draw the outline of the object on this kind of a surface similarly to shadow theatre.

5. Of a screen memory (*Deckerinnerung*), Lacan uses the French translation *le souvenir-écran* (Lacan 1994, 157).

6. The concept of documentarism is problematic. If the photograph has an indexical relationship with the object that is located before the optics, the photograph is a kind of a document of something. In this regard, all photographs are documentary and hence the expression documentary photograph becomes tautological.

    The term documentary was used for the first time as a feature that characterizes the photograph by English movie producer John Grierson when he wrote a review of Robert Flaherty's anthropological film *Moana*. The review was published in the *New York Sun* in February 1926. According to Grierson, *Moana* "had documentary value, because it was a visual account of the lives of Polynesian youth". Grierson defined documentarism as "the creative treatment of actuality" (see Hardy 1966). Two years later the term surfaced in France. Critic Christian Zervos linked it with the photographs of Eugéne Atget and André Kertész. Documentarism did not expand into a concept that characterized the photograph more extensively before the 1930s (Solomon-Godeau 1991, 299).

CHAPTER 4—READING PICTURES

1. Watching TV does correlate with the development of children's literacy (Eskola 1991, 67). However, the connection between watching TV and the average level of literacy is not significant (Linnakylä 1995, 117–121), and varies between different countries and age groups. For example, in France, the USA and Germany there was a clear connection among nine-year-olds: the more frequently children watched TV, the poorer their level of literacy was. In Finland and other Nordic countries, children of the same age group who watched TV relatively often, 3–4 hours per day, performed best in literacy tests; whereas children who watched TV over 5 hours a day

did not succeed as well. In the age group of 14-year-olds, the situation was totally different: the group that watched TV less than one hour a day did the best in reading tests. (*Ibid.*, 120; on the problematics of literacy and TV watching see also e.g. Neuman 1991.)

2. Messaris does not make a distinction between a picture and a photograph. In the following, I apply Messaris's thinking about the picture in general to the photograph where possible.

REFERENCES

ARGYLE, M., and M. COOK 1976. *Gaze and mutual gaze*. London: Cambridge University Press.

ARNHEIM, R. 1969. *Visual thinking*. Berkeley and Los Angeles: University of California Press.

BACK, L., and V. QUAADE 1993. Dream utopias, nightmare realities: Imaging race and culture withing the world of Benetton. *Third Text* 22: 65–80.

BARTHES, R. 1993. *Camera Lucida: Reflections on photography*. Trans. by RICHARD HOWARD. London: Vintage.

————1987. The photographic message. In *Image, music, text*, essays selected and translated by STEPHEN HEATH, 15–31. London: Fontana.

BARTON, D. 1994. *Literacy: an introduction to the ecology of written language*. Oxford and Cambridge: Blackwell.

BAUDRILLARD, J. 1983. *Simulations*. Trans. by PAUL FOSS, PAUL PATTON and PHILIP BEITCHMAN. New York: Semiotext(e).

————1988a. *The ecstasy of communication*. Trans. by BERNARD and CAROLINE SCHUTZE, edited by SYLVÈRE LOTRINGER. New York: Semiotext(e).

————1988b. *Selected writings*. Ed. by MARK POSTER. Stanford: Stanford University Press.

BAZIN, A. 1967. The ontology of photographic image. In *What is cinema?*, essays selected and translated by HUGH GRAY, 9–16. Berkeley and Los Angeles: University of California Press.

BERGER, J. 1977. *Ways of seeing*. London: BBC and Penguin.

BOGLE, D. 1996. *Toms, coons, mulattoes, mammies and bucks: An interpretive history of blacks in American films*. New York: Continuum.

BRADEN, S. 1983. *Committing photography*. London: Pluto Press.

BRYSON, N. 1988. The gaze in the expanded field. In *Vision and visuality*, ed. H. FOSTER, 87–108. Seattle: Bay Press.

BURBULES, N. C. 1998. Rhetorics of the web: hyperreading and critical literacy. In *Page to screen: Taking literacy into the electronic era*, ed. I. SNYDER, 102–122. London and New York: Routledge.

BÜRGER, P. 1984. *Theory of the avant-garde*. Minnesota: University of Minnesota Press.

BURGOON, J. K., BULLER, D. B., and G. W. WOODALL. 1996. *Nonverbal communication: The unspoken dialogue*. New York: McGraw-Hill.

BURNETT, R. 1995. *Cultures of vision: Images, media and the imaginary*. Bloomington and Indianapolis: Indiana University Press.

CATALANO, J. S. 1985. *A commentary on Jean-Paul Sartre's 'Being and nothingness'.* Chicago: University of Chicago Press.

CRARY, J. 1988. Modernizing vision. In *Vision and visuality,* ed. H. FOSTER, 29–44. Seattle: Bay Press.

———1990. *Techniques of the observer: On vision and modernity in the nineteenth century.* Cambridge: MIT Press.

DAGUERRE, L. J. M. 1980. Daguerrotype. In *Classic essays on photography,* ed. A. TRACHTENBERG, 11–13. New Haven: Leete's Island Books.

DE SAUSSURE, F. 1983. *Course in general linguistics.* Trans. by RICHARD HARRIS. London: Duckworth.

DEBES, J. 1986. Foreword. In *Visual literacy connections to thinking and writing,* by R. SINATRA, vii–viii. Illinois: Charles S. Thomas.

DEBORD, G. 1987. *Society of the spectacle.* (Translator's name not mentioned.) London: Rebel Press, Aim Publications.

ECO, U. 1982. Critique of the image. In *Thinking photography,* ed. V. BURGIN, 32–38. London: Macmillan.

ELKINS, J. 2003. *Visual studies: A skeptical introduction.* New York and London: Routledge.

ESKOLA, K. 1991. Miten suomalaiset käyttävät lukutaitoaan? (How do Finns use their literacy?). In *Toimiva lukutaito,* ed. M. HILTUNEN and M-L. TOUKONEN, 30–45. Helsinki: UNESCO.

FAIRCLOUGH, N. 1995. *Media discourse.* London: Edvard Arnold.

FISKE, J. 1990. *Introduction to communication studies.* Second Edition. London and New York: Routledge.

FORCEVILLE, C. 1994. Pictorial metaphor in advertisements. *Metaphor and Symbolic Activity* (9)1: 1–29.

FOUCAULT, M. 1977. *Discipline and punish: The birth of the prison.* Trans. by ALAN SHERIDAN. New York: Pantheon Books.

———1986. *Power/Knowledge: Selected interviews and other writings 1972–1977.* Ed. by COLIN GORDON. Suffolk: The Harvester Press.

———1989. *Archaelogy of knowledge.* Trans. by A. M. SHERIDAN. London: Routledge.

FREUD, S. 1992. Screen memories. In *Standard Edition of the complete psychological works of Sigmund Freud,* ed. JAMES STRACHEY et al., Vol III, 301–322. London: Hogarth Press.

GILLIAN, R. 2001. *Visual methodologies: An introduction to the interpretation of visual materials.* London: Sage.

GILSTER, P. 1997. *Digital literacy.* New York: John Wiley & Sons.

GRIFFIN, R. E., GIBBS, W. J., and B. WIEGMAN (eds.) 1999. *Visual literacy in an information age.* International Visual Literacy Association, IVLA (no publisher's location).

GRIFFIN, R. E., GIBBS, W. J., and V. S. WILLIAMS (eds.) 2000. *Natural vistas: Visual literacy & the world around us.* International Visual Literacy Association, IVLA (no publisher's location).

HALL, S. 1986. Encoding/decoding. In *Culture, media, language: Working papers in cultural studies, 1972–79,* ed. S. HALL et al., 128–138. London: Hutchinson.

———1997. The spectacle of the Other. In *Representation: Cultural representations and signifying practices,* ed. S. HALL, 223–290. London: Sage and Open University.

HARDY, F. 1966. *Grierson on documentary.* London: Faber and Faber.

HAUG, W. F. 1984. Die Camera obscura des Bewusstseins Kritik der Subjekt/Objekt-Artikulation im Marxismus. In *Die Camera Obscura der Ideologie*, ed. W. F. HAUG, 9–96. Berlin: Argument-Verlag.

HIRSCH, E. D., JR., KETT, J. F., and J. TREFIL. 1988. *The dictionary of cultural literacy*. Boston: Houghton Mifflin Company.

HIRSCH, E. D. JR. 1987. *Cultural literacy: What every American needs to know*. Boston: Houghton Mifflin Company.

HOLLAND, P. 1997. 'Sweet it is to scan...'. In *Photography: A critical introduction*, ed. L. WELLS, 103–150. London and New York: Routledge.

HUHTAMO, E. 1997. *Elävän kuvan arkeologia* (Archaeology of moving images). Helsinki: Finnish Broadcasting Company.

JAY, M. 1988. Scopic regimes of modernity. In *Vision and visuality*, ed. H. FOSTER, 3–20. Seattle: Bay Press.

———1993. *Downcast eyes: The denigration of vision in twentieth-century French thought*. Berkeley and Los Angeles: University of California Press.

JENKS, C. 1995. The centrality of the eye in western culture. In *Visual culture*, ed. C. JENKS, 1–25. London and New York: Routledge.

JULKUNEN, R. 2000. Kertooko ulkonäkö pätevyyden? (Does appearance correspond to competence?). *Helsingin Sanomat* 24.12.2000, A5.

KALANTI, T. 1990. Visuaalisista ja verbaalisista koodeista (On visual and verbal codes). *Synteesi* 9:2–3.

KOFMAN, S. 1998. *Camera obscura of ideology*. Trans. by WILL STRAW. London: The Athlone Press.

KRESS, G., and T. VAN LEEUWEN. 1996. *Reading images: The grammar of visual design*. London and New York: Routledge.

LACAN, J. 1977a. *Écrits: A selection*. Trans. by ALAN SHERIDAN. London: Tavistock Publications.

———1977b. *The four fundamental concepts of psycho-analysis*. Trans. by ALAN SHERIDAN. London: Penguin Books.

———1994. *Le Séminaire IV. La Relation l'objet (1956–1957)*. Paris: Seuil.

LEHTONEN, M. 1994. *Kyklooppi ja kojootti: subjekti 1600–1900 -lukujen kulttuuri- ja kirjallisuusteoriassa* (The Cyclope and the coyote: Subject in cultural and literary theories from the 17th to the 18th century). Tampere: Vastapaino.

LINNAKYLÄ, P. 1995. *Lukutaidolla maailmankartalle: kansainvälinen lukutaitotutkimus Suomessa* (From literacy to the world map: International literacy research in Finland). Jyväskylä: University of Jyväskylä.

LISTER, M. (ed.) 1995. *The photographic image in digital culture*. London and New York: Routledge.

MACEY, D. 1988. *Lacan in contexts*. London: Verso.

MANOVICH, L. 1997. The paradoxes of digital photography. In *Photography after photography: Memory and representation in the digital age*, ed. H. AMELUNXEN et al., 57–65. Amsterdam: OPA.

MASTERMAN, L. 1985. *Teaching the media*. London: Comedia.

MERCER, K., and I. JULIEN. 1994. Black masculinity and the politics of race. In *Welcome to the jungle*, ed. K. MERCER. London and New York: Routledge.

MESSARIS, P. 1994. *Visual "literacy": Image, mind, and reality*. Oxford: Westview Press.

MIRZOEFF, N. 1999. *An introduction to visual culture*. London and New York: Routledge.

MITCHELL, W. J. 1992. *The reconfigured eye: Visual truth in the post-photographic era*. Cambridge: MIT Press.

NEUMAN, S. B. 1991. *Literacy in the television age: The myth of the TV effect*. Norwood: Ablex Publishing Corporation.

NÖTH, W. 1995. *Handbook of semiotics*. Bloomington and Indianapolis: Indiana University Press.

PEIRCE, C. S. 1932. *Elements of logic. Collected papers, vol. II* . Ed. by C. HARTSHORNE and P. WEISS. Cambridge: Harvard University Press.

PETT, D. W. 1988. *History of the international visual literacy association: One person's perspective* (www. ivla.org/organization/history.htm, consulted 7/2002).

PLANT, S. 1992. *The most radical gesture: The situationist international in a postmodern age*. London and New York: Routledge.

POSTER, M. 2002. Visual studies as media studies. *Journal of Visual Culture* (1)1, 67–70.

POTTER, J. W. 1998. *Media literacy*. London: Sage.

ROSE, G. 2001. *Visual methodologies: An introduction to the interpretation of visual materials*. London: Sage.

SARTRE, J.-P. 1992. *Being and nothingness: A phenomenological essay on ontology*. Trans. by H. E. BARNES. New York: Washington Square Press.

SEPPÄNEN, J. 2000. Young people, researchers and Benetton: Contest interpretations of a Benetton advertisement picture. *Nordicom Review* (22)1, 85–96.

SILVERMAN, K. 1996. *The threshold of the visible world*. London and New York: Routledge.

SIMMEL, G. 1968. *Soziologie: Untersuchungen über die Formen der Vergesellschaftung*. Berlin: Duncker & Humblot.

———1993. Soziologie der Sinne. In *Gesamtausgabe, Band. 8. Bd. II: Aufsätze und Abhandlungen 1901–1908*, 113–146. Frankfurt am Main: Suhrkamp.

SINATRA, R. 1986. *Visual literacy connections to thinking, reading and writing*. Illinois: Charles C. Thomas.

SIVENIUS, P. 1997. Silmän kääntö (Turning of the eye). *Tiedotustutkimus* (20)3, 49–57.

SLATER, D. 1995a. Domestic photography and digital culture. In *The Photographic image in digital culture*, ed. M. LISTER, 129–146. London and New York: Routledge.

———1995b. Photography and modern vision: The spectacle of 'Natural Magic'. In *Visual culture*, ed. C. JENKS, 218–237. London and New York: Routledge.

SNYDER, I. 1998. Page to screen. In *Page to screen: taking literacy into the electronic era*, ed. I. SNYDER, xx–xxxvi. London and New York: Routledge.

SOL. Suomi osaa lukea (The Finns can read). Report 4:2000. Helsinki: Ministry of Education.

SOLOMON-GODEAU, A. 1991. *Photography at the dock: Essays on photographic history, institutions and practices*. Minneapolis: University of Minnesota Press.

SONESSON, G. 1989. *Pictorial concepts: Inquiries into the semiotic heritage and its relevance for the analysis of the visual world*. Lund: Lund University Press.

SPENCE, J. 1995. *Cultural sniping: The art of transgression*. London and New York: Routledge.

STURKEN, M., and L. CARTWRIGHT. 2001. *Practices of looking: An introduction to visual culture*. Oxford: Oxford University Press.

TAGG, J. 1988. *The burden of representation: Essays on photographies and histories*. London: Macmillan.

THEUNISSEN, M. 1984. *The Other: Studies in the social ontology of Husserl, Heidegger, Sartre and Buber*. Trans. by C. MACANN. Cambridge: MIT Press.

TICHO, G. R. 1967. On self-analysis. *International Journal of Psycho-Analysis.* 48: 308–318.

TUDOR, A. 1999. *Decoding culture: Theory and method in cultural studies.* London: Sage.

VERHOEVEN, L. (ed.) 1994. *Functional literacy: Theoretical issues and educational implications.* Amsterdam and Philadelphia: John Benjamin's Publishing Company.

VIRTANEN, K. 2000. Muodot kunniaan! (Respect curves!). *Me Naiset* 10.11.2000, 70–72.

WALKER, J. A., and S. CHAPLIN. 1997. *Visual culture: An introduction.* Manchester: Manchester University Press.

WEBER, S. 1991. *Return to Freud: Jacques Lacan's dislocation of psycho-analysis.* Trans. by MICHAEL LEVINE. Cambridge: Cambridge University Press.

WEINSTEIN, D., and M. WEINSTEIN. 1984. On the visual constitution of society: the contributions of Georg Simmel and Jean-Paul Sartre to a sociology of senses. *History of European Ideas* (5)4, 349–362.

WILLIS, P. 1990. *Common culture: Symbolic work at play in the everyday cultures of the young.* With S. JONES, J. CANAAN and G. HURD. Boulder and San Francisco: Westview Press.

WINTEROWD, W. R. 1989. *The culture and politics of literacy.* Oxford: Oxford University Press.

Colin Lankshear, Michele Knobel,
Chris Bigum, & Michael Peters
General Editors

New literacies and new knowledges are being invented "in the streets"
as people from all walks of life wrestle with new technologies, shift-
ing values, changing institutions, and new structures of personality
and temperament emerging in a global informational age. These new literacies and ways of knowing remain absent from classrooms. Many education administrators, teachers, teacher educators, and academics seem
largely unaware of them. Others actively oppose them. Yet, they increasingly shape the engagements and worlds of young people in societies like our own. The *New Literacies and Digital Epistemologies* series
will explore this terrain with a view to informing educational theory
and practice in constructively critical ways.

For further information about the series and submitting manu-
scripts, please contact:

Michele Knobel & Colin Lankshear
Montclair State University
Dept of Education
210 Finley Hall
Montclair, NJ 07043
michele@coatepec.net

To order other books in this series, please contact our Customer
Service Department at:

(800) 770-LANG (within the U.S.)
(212) 647-7706 (outside the U.S.)
(212) 647-7707 FAX

Or browse online by series at:

www.peterlang.com